Courage Is Contagious

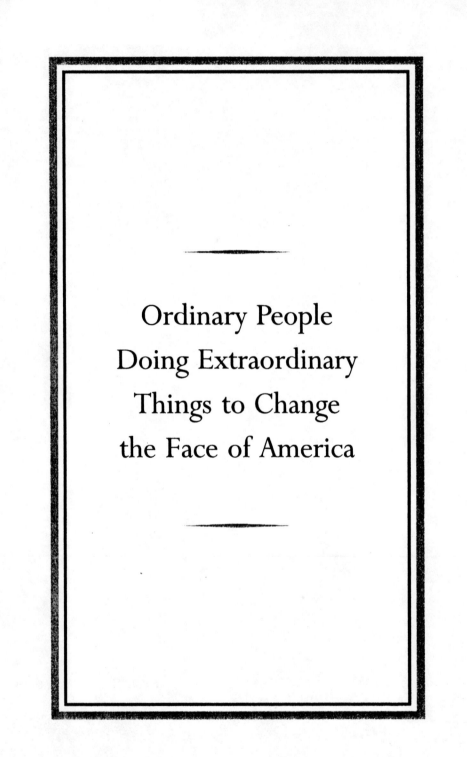

Ordinary People
Doing Extraordinary
Things to Change
the Face of America

JOHN KASICH

Courage Is Contagious

MAIN STREET BOOKS

DOUBLEDAY

New York   London   Toronto   Sydney   Auckland

A Main Street Book
PUBLISHED BY DOUBLEDAY
a division of Random House, Inc.
1540 Broadway, New York, New York 10036

MAIN STREET BOOKS, DOUBLEDAY, and the portrayal of a building with a tree
are trademarks of Doubleday, a division of Random House, Inc.

Courage Is Contagious was originally published in hardcover
by Doubleday in 1998. The Main Street Books edition is
published by arrangement with Doubleday.

The Library of Congress has cataloged the Doubleday
hardcover edition as follows:

Kasich, John.
Courage is contagious: ordinary people doing extraordinary things
to change the face of America / John Kasich.
p.   cm.
1. Voluntarism—United States—Case studies.   2. Helping behavior—
United States—Case studies.   I. Title.
HN90.V64K38   1998
361.3'7'0973—dc21   98-16244
CIP

ISBN 0-385-49148-4

For My Parents
John and Anne Kasich

CONTENTS

Contents

ACKNOWLEDGMENTS

I would like to thank several people for their advice and assistance on this book. My wife Karen gave me her encouragement and many helpful suggestions. She truly is my inspiration.

My friend Ron Hartman accompanied me on some of my trips, read the manuscript, and as always was generous with his time and his wisdom.

My literary agent, Ron Goldfarb, worked with me to develop the concept of the book and in many other ways helped bring it to life. He has become a great friend.

My editor at Doubleday, Roger Scholl, was a source of good advice and constant encouragement and enthusiasm as the manuscript took shape.

Finally, I want to thank Patrick Anderson for his invaluable assistance. Pat worked to understand my feelings about the people in this book. He and I worked countless hours to put those feelings on paper. I hope this book will touch your heart. If it does, Pat deserves great credit. Most important, I made a new friend.

INTRODUCTION

T HIS BOOK is about some of my heroes.
They are not my fellow members of Congress,
although I admire many of them.

These heroes don't hold public office. In most cases,
they're not well known outside the communities where
they live and work.

They are people who bring life and hope to the aged,
the homeless, the helpless, the sick and dying. They do
God's work on this earth, often in the face of senseless
obstacles put in their way by government.

They are part of the new volunteerism in America,
and I believe that if anyone can save our country from violence, cynicism and despair they can. There are millions of
them working all across America, in every community. I'm
lucky to have gotten to know just a few of them.

What these heroes are doing is tremendously important. I've served in Congress since 1983, and I'm increasingly frustrated there. Although Congress has great power,
I believe we have entered an era in which we have largely
exhausted the usefulness of lawmaking. We pass laws but
too often nothing changes—if anyone benefits, it's mostly
lawyers and bureaucrats.

I'm not anti-government. I'm a blue-collar kid from

McKees Rocks, Pennsylvania. My dad delivered mail and often told me how much the New Deal meant to working people in the 1930s. Later, in the 1960s, we needed civil rights legislation and Medicare. But now it's time for the pendulum to swing back. Government has an important role to play but it must be limited. Instead, government has gotten too big, has become too intrusive into people's lives. Too often now it's part of the problem instead of part of the solution. Too often, instead of helping the heroes I celebrate in this book, it hobbles them with heavy-handed regulations, red tape and boneheaded tax policies.

It isn't just government. Big institutions are part of the problem too—both big business and big labor. Too often they care only about self-interest. They become partners with government in grinding people down. Too often our most talented lawyers are hired guns for special interests, and our system of justice is stacked against ordinary people. Too often the legal system is used not to search for truth or justice but as a means of blackmail. The individual is under great pressure to settle a case to avoid huge legal costs or even bankruptcy. This isn't how it ought to be.

What can average Americans do to bring about social change? The answer is, we can do a lot, if we are willing to set goals and work for them. Too often we suffer from what I call the home run syndrome. We think that unless we hit a home run—or win the lottery or write a best seller—we might as well not try. We aren't interested in small victories.

I believe we have to reject the home run syndrome and believe in the power of one, the ability of each of us to make a difference. The people in this book believe in taking small steps to change society. They save one child at a time. They comfort one sick or dying person at a time. They tutor and teach at-risk students one at a time. They build our economy one job at a time. Their determined spadework is more effective than many government programs in helping those who need and deserve our help. Government doesn't have a heart or a soul—government is a machine. There are some jobs it does well, but saving the spirit and soul of America isn't one of them.

At heart, this book is a celebration, not only of the people I write about, but of millions of others who are doing good work. But we must not just sit back and applaud these heroes. We need to join them, because there should be many more of them.

You don't always hear much about these people because they don't seek publicity and because the media often seem to prefer scandal and gossip over stories about people who are quietly doing good.

In this book I'll talk about just a few of the unsung heroes I've met.

I'll talk about Gretchen Buchenholz, who works to save the lives of babies born with AIDS—and took on the state of New York when it was refusing to identify infants with AIDS, because it had decided that a mother's privacy was more important than her child's life.

I'll discuss Albert Lexie, a retarded man who for years has been shining shoes in Pittsburgh and giving his tips to a hospital fund for children—more than $40,000 so far, one pair of shoes at a time.

I'll introduce Dr. Jack McConnell, who retired to the luxury community of Hilton Head Island, South Carolina, but soon found himself bored with golf and recruited hundreds of retired doctors and nurses to treat people who have no health insurance.

I'll describe Amber and Bobbi Coffman, a mother and daughter who every week, helped by teenage volunteers, feed hundreds of homeless people in Maryland.

I'll introduce Michael Christensen, a circus clown who out of personal tragedy created a national program to bring joy to thousands of sick and dying children.

Was it hard to find heroes? Here's how hard. One chilly October night my wife Karen and I and some friends attended the Rolling Stones concert at the new Jack Kent Cooke Stadium outside Washington. After the opening act, Karen and I went to get a hot dog. This book was the furthest thing from my mind, but as we waited in line I noticed how efficient and enthusiastic the fellows operating the hot dog stand were. When we reached the front of the line, I started a conversation with the man who waited on me. He turned out to be Thomas D. Jefferson, an auditor with the U.S. Department of Transportation's Office of Inspector General. Tom explained that he and his colleagues are members of the Prince Georges County, Maryland, graduate chapter of Omega Psi Phi, an African-American fraternity whose members stay together after college to raise money for scholarships for deserving youngsters and other worthwhile causes. There are dozens of these fraternities, with tens of thousands of members, doing outstanding volunteer work all over America.

Want to find a hero? Go buy a hot dog.

Once a teenage girl who had befriended children with multiple handicaps told me how much fun they had together.

"Does it ever bother you?" I asked.

"What do you mean?"

"Most people would run from children with all those problems," I said.

"I think they're special," she explained.

Of course, she was right—those children are special. What she might not have understood is that so is she.

I've come to believe that everyone has a gift to con-

14

tribute. Some people find it early in life, some when they are older, and unfortunately some never do. In Oklahoma City, talking with hospice workers, I met a remarkable woman named Polly Keenan, who after a successful career as a real estate agent became a nurse. "I have a gift for being with dying people," she told me. Polly was fortunate enough to discover her gift, and each of us must try to find ours. Releasing the power of these individual gifts can have a huge impact on our society.

As much as I admire people like Polly Keenan, I know that we're not all like that. She has a special gift, and it's not mine and may not be yours. But we have gifts, too, if we'll use them. We can't all be Mother Teresa but we all can do something. We can visit the woman down the street whose husband died. We can pick up trash by the side of the road. We can give a kind word or a sandwich to a homeless person. In 1981, one of the people I have profiled in this book, Karen Olson, impulsively bought a sandwich for a homeless woman; today, Karen heads a program that serves thousands of homeless people all over America.

You don't even have to volunteer to serve others—you can seek justice in the workplace. Both labor and management can look beyond their immediate interests to the public interest. Employers can provide health benefits even when they aren't required to. Labor leaders can use reason and restraint. We can treat our subordinates with consideration and make sure we're fair to women and minorities. At the end of the day, each of us can ask if we've helped make the world a better place for our kids—or someone else's. Cheryl Krueger, one of the heroes in this book, is an example of the kind of boss who can make a better world as well as a profit.

Whether in the workplace or as volunteers, we must

have the courage to care, because that kind of courage is contagious.

I met Hanna Hawkins one day in House Majority Leader Dick Armey's office. Hanna is a wiry woman who operates Children of Mine, an after-school program that serves more than a hundred children each weekday afternoon in the Anacostia section of Washington, D.C. Anacostia, a few miles south of the U.S. Capitol, is the sort of neighborhood tourists never see and many cab drivers won't take you to. A dozen years ago Hanna was a drug counselor; then she decided she wanted to focus her energies on helping children whose lives were devastated by their parents' drug abuse. She started taking children into her home, then was able to obtain the use of a larger house. She and her volunteers help children with their homework, teach them to sew and use computers, take them on field trips and find them used clothing, and serve an early dinner that may be the best or even the only meal they receive that day.

All this is done by volunteers and with the private donations that dribble in. ("God always has a ram in the bush!" she says.) Hanna doesn't have much use for government programs. For a while she was receiving food from a Department of Agriculture program, but one of its inspectors came by and was shocked that she was serving food at two-thirty in the afternoon. "You aren't supposed to serve it before three-thirty," he declared. He was even more shocked when he learned that she let children take leftovers home. "I told him I'd always feed a hungry child, no matter what time it was," Hawkins says, "and that I won't ever throw away good food." Fortunately the inspector never came back.

Hanna urgently needs more volunteers. "Everyone should donate just one hour a week to some cause," she says. "Think what a difference that would make. The volunteers I get the most from are the people who are busiest. The ones who aren't doing anything can always find a reason not to do anything. 'I'm busy,' they say. Busy doing what?"

The truth is that millions of us could donate an hour a week—or more—and what a difference those millions of hours could make. It's no good to stand on the sidelines and complain. If we want a better America we have to roll up our sleeves and make it happen. This book is about people who are doing that, setting a standard, showing us the way. I hope you enjoy meeting them. More importantly, I hope they move you to action. We can all be heroes if we only have the courage to try.

Courage Is Contagious

The Definition
of Courage

Bobby and Eric Krenzke

We need courage in America, the courage to take charge of our lives, to confront the hard issues, to build a better future. I have known many courageous people in my life, but none more than two boys, brothers, who faced death and never cried, never complained, never lost their love for their family and friends or their faith in God. At those times when you think your life is difficult, give some thought to Eric and Bobby Krenzke, to the courage and grit and hope they showed during their short lives. And to the courage of their parents too.

I T WAS THROUGH the Special Wish Foundation that I met Eric and Bobby Krenzke. Ramona Fickle started the foundation in 1982 to grant the "special wishes" of dying children. "People ask if I had a child die," Ramona says. "No, that wasn't it. My husband and I have six wonderful children. I guess I felt like I had to pay some dues. I was working as the executive secretary to a college president and I decided to volunteer at a hospice. I wanted to work with dying children but they had no special program for children. I saw that while dying was awful for the adults it was even more awful for the children. Sometimes they would want things, and if their families couldn't afford them it would break your heart. So I decided to start Special Wish. Often, I've wondered how the parents of dying children carry on, day after day. I guess the answer is, they have to."

Ramona estimates that by now the foundation, which is based in Columbus, Ohio, has granted more than three thousand wishes for young people. Two of them were for Bobby and Eric Krenzke. Eric had wished for a trip to Disney World, which is what many children want. But Bobby, the older and more bookish of the brothers, had a different plan. He wanted to come to Washington and meet President Clinton and see Congress, the Supreme Court, the FBI and the Hard Rock Cafe. Bobby was all of nine then, but he loved to read about history and politics and he knew that our government has three branches and he decided he wanted to see all three for himself.

For some reason, when they arrived in Washington in September 1994, the Krenzke family had trouble getting tickets for a tour of the Capitol, and they called my office for help. When I heard about the family, I invited them to lunch. They were from Hilliard, Ohio, just a short drive from where I live.

The first time we met, Bobby was sitting in a wheelchair in the Capitol, wearing a bicycle helmet and red, white and blue pants. Eric, who was five, was also in a wheelchair and wearing a helmet. They were in wheelchairs because they were too weak to walk; the helmets were to protect them if they fell. Even though I knew the boys were sick, it was a shock to see them like that.

Bobby and Eric and their parents, Pam and Lind Krenzke, met me for lunch in the House dining room. We were all a little stiff at first. Then Eric dropped his grilled cheese sandwich onto the floor, and when his family razzed him about it we loosened up. The Krenzkes had long since learned to use laughter as a way of dealing with the reality they faced—the four of them did a lot of razzing.

During lunch I teased the boys a little by asking how they'd gotten to be so smart—for they were clearly unusually bright, well-informed, articulate kids. They had their answer ready: "Because our parents read to us!" They were blessed with wonderful parents. Lind, a big, bearded man, is a computer systems analyst. Pam is in charge of adult literacy training for the Columbus public schools.

After lunch I took the boys onto the floor of the House of Representatives, where Congressmen crowded around to meet them. Bobby had deliberately chosen to wear his red, white and blue pants with stars and stripes on them so no one would miss him. Bobby never minded attention—he was right at home among all those politicians. There was a vote in progress and I told Bobby to keep his eye on the board that recorded votes, because when it got to 218 my side would have won. But Congressmen kept coming to meet him, obscuring his view. He finally said, "Could you get out of the way, please, I can't see the vote count!"

At the end of the vote he informed me, "By the way, John, your side just lost!"

That day was the beginning of our friendship. At first I was closer to Bobby, but over time I grew close to Eric as well. Both boys suffered from dystonia, a rare, genetic neurological disorder. With dystonia, the brain can't get all of its messages to the muscles. That means that some people with the disease can't eat. Some can't walk or talk. Sometimes their hearts beat too fast. Barring a miracle, it is almost always fatal.

Eric was diagnosed with dystonia in 1990, when he was eighteen months old; he responded well to treatment and the disease went into remission. Bobby showed no symptoms at first. The doctors told the Krenzkes that if a child reaches seven with no sign of the disease there is a good chance he won't develop it. Sadly, in February 1994, when Bobby was eight, he was diagnosed with the disease. For both boys to be victims of the disease, as Pam once told me, was a parent's worst nightmare.

Bobby was a skinny kid with an impish face and a disposition to match. Before his illness he was a normal boy, a Cub Scout who loved to run and ride his bike and roller-skate. Soon he had lost a great deal of his physical energy—although never his mental energy—as well as thirty-five pounds, and much of the use of his hands and digestive system.

I go home to Columbus almost every weekend, to see

the people who elected me to Congress and to see Karen Waldbillig, who is now my wife. Karen and I started visiting Bobby on the weekends. I took him to a Power Rangers rock concert, and to a museum, and we watched his favorite TV shows, "The Little Rascals" and "The Simpsons." We both loved the Simpsons: there was a lot of Bart in Bobby and, to my chagrin, he insisted there was a lot of Homer in me. During the week I would call him frequently from Washington. It didn't matter how late I called. Because Bobby didn't sleep much, he kept very unusual hours.

Seeing Bobby was never a matter of sympathy or doing him a favor. It was one of friendship. If any favors were done, in fact, he did them for me. In Washington, I inhabit a world of compromise; back home, Bobby reminded me what real courage is.

We never had any trouble relating. Bobby once told his mother, "Mom, John's just a kid in a Congressman's body." We made a lot of dumb jokes back and forth, and when I made one he would roll his eyes comically. He had a great sense of humor, even though it hurt him physically to laugh. Sometimes he would ask Karen for a kiss, and once he confessed to her he was trying to make me jealous. Jealous? I admired his good taste.

Bobby was nine going on forty. He knew he was going to die, but he never complained, never whined, never cried. Bobby was the definition of courage. "Bobby, you're doing so well, let's make a deal," I once kidded him. "When I'm dying, will you promise to come help me?" He grinned and said, "Shake on it, John!"

He was always reading, always watching educational shows on TV, always trying to learn. He was studying the dictionary to learn new words right up to the end. Sometimes we would spend an hour going over the capitals of all the countries in the world. He just wanted to make sure he had them right. If he had lived, I think Bobby would have been a scholar or teacher; he had a first-rate mind and a true thirst for knowledge.

I think one reason I became friends with Bobby was that I had lost my parents so suddenly. One night in August 1987 they were leaving a restaurant in McKees Rocks when a car driven by a drunk driver crashed into their car. My father died instantly and my mother died a few hours later. There was no chance to say goodbye; these two hardworking, God-fearing, decent people, who had sacrificed so much for me, were just suddenly gone. A tragedy like that can destroy you, or it can be an opportunity to grow. God blessed me and I grew. It caused a rebirth of my religious faith. Their deaths made me more sensitive to others, and made me want to help people deal with their tragedies when I could. Many people helped me through my own difficult time, with only the expectation that I in turn would help others when I could. When I met Bobby and Eric and their parents, I wanted to help. At the very least I could be their friend and when the end came I could say a decent goodbye.

By November 1994, just two months after we met, Bobby had become so weak that he was placed in a hospice. It was clear that he didn't have long to live. In February he wrote me a letter:

Dear John: This is important. This next part is kind of a secret. I usually talk to my stuffed animals. If I die, mostly I want you to say something at my funeral. I might not die at this age. I'm still myself, but I'm weaker than myself. But if I die, you can tell everybody how nice a kid I am, that I'm smart, and that I'm funny. I love when you come to visit me. It was fun watching the movie with you.

27

ry tired. Are you taking care of yourself? I
e. That's all I have to say this time. Love,

That letter was typical of Bobby: optimistic, realistic
and caring, all at the same time. He was worried about *me*.
Nonetheless, I gave him a hard time about the letter. I told
him that I'd speak at his funeral, but I didn't need him to
tell me what to say. He quickly shot back the observation
that I probably *could* use a little help.

We talked about religion some, although once he told
me, "John, don't start the God thing, it's squared away.
It's all worked out. Don't worry about it." He understood
that God was going to take him home.

My forty-third birthday took place on May 13. Bobby
knew it was my birthday and asked me to come see him.
When I entered his room he was waiting in bed with a
package in his arms. He was very thin and weak. He said,
"This is for you, John." The package contained his most
prized possession, the football that Ohio State's legendary
tailback Archie Griffin had given him; he wanted me to
have it. No one ever received a more precious gift.

Bobby died two days later, just eight months after I
first met him. As he had requested, I spoke at his funeral at
the Atonement Lutheran Church in Columbus. When they
were making up the program, Pam asked me if I should be
listed as a eulogist. That title seemed too fancy—I could
imagine what Bobby would have said about that. I told
her, "Just say I was a buddy." So that's how I was listed:
John Kasich, Buddy.

The point I tried to make at Bobby's funeral was not
just that he was bright and funny and brave, and that he
loved his parents and his brother very much. All that was
true, but my real message was that nothing that any of us

did for Bobby was as important as what he did for us. God gave him to us and he inspired us—his family, his friends, his classmates—and gave us courage and hope. Then one day God said, "I can't heal you, Bobby, I need to bring you home." We didn't have to mourn him, because his pain was over. He was happy, he was with God, and yet he'd left a piece of himself behind in all of us.

When Pam and Lind adopted their daughter Betsy in February 1996, Karen and I were among her godparents. In December 1996 Karen and I accompanied Pam, Lind, Eric and Betsy to a Special Wish Foundation Christmas party. Most of the children there were terminally ill, yet it was an evening filled with happiness. The Krenzkes and other families with sick or dying children will tell you there's nothing you can do to take away their pain. You use your time and money and energy trying to make the child get better. When getting better is no longer an option, you just try to be brave. For these families, being together gave them strength and comfort. Eating pizza, drinking soda pop and playing pinball and video games brought at least a temporary healing. That night Eric beat me at pinball two times out of three—he loved that.

Early in 1997 Eric went into a decline. His heart grew weaker and he spent most of the time sleeping. A friend and I visited the Krenzkes on a Sunday afternoon in mid-July. He'd been honored at Hilliard's Fourth of July parade a week before, but since then he'd been sleeping almost around the clock. When we arrived, Eric was on the sofa, under a color photograph of himself and Bobby, with an oxygen tube in his nose. Mike Duffey, a college student and family friend, sat beside him, and Pam and Lind were close by. Eighteen-month-old Betsy was toddling about.

Eric perked up when I arrived and—over his parents' protests—insisted on demonstrating a ninja kick he'd mastered. He spoke in a whisper but he had a lot to say. He announced that he had a girlfriend named Kate who came to see him, but added, "No, John, I haven't kissed her yet." He showed my friend some animals he'd sculpted out of clay and some of his watercolors. One of them was his vision of heaven, with stars representing friends of his who were already there. He was thinking a lot about heaven in those final months. Once he told me he hoped there were trees in heaven, because his illness had kept him from climbing all the trees he wanted to climb on earth.

When my friend complimented the drawings, he insisted on giving him a Beanie Baby, one of dozens that people had given to Eric. He even sang for us, the theme song from the "Mr. Rogers" TV show. After a while Pam became concerned that Eric was wearing himself out and tried to get him back onto the sofa. When he protested, Betsy began to cry—anything that hurt Eric hurt her too. Finally, Eric settled down and we said our goodbyes. "He's lived his life to the fullest," Pam said as we parted.

Karen and I went to see Eric twice more that summer. Each time he was weaker and it was clear that the end was near. On August 31, Pam called to tell me that Eric was dead.

On September 6, I returned to the Atonement Lutheran Church, this time for a celebration of Eric's life. I was one of the pallbearers. The music on the program included not only "Amazing Grace" and "Love Lifted Me," but "The Scooby Doo Theme" and "Take Me Out to the Ballgame."

The program reproduced this handwritten note: "Gone to see Bobby. See you soon. Love, Eric."

I found that Eric's death hit me even harder than Bobby's had. I guess it was the finality of knowing that they both were gone.

I once asked Pam how she and Lind were able to keep on in the face of such an ordeal. She said, "We recognize the value of the children. We recognize that they are gifts that we've been given. We take each day as it comes. We have no other choice. Are we sad sometimes? Yes. Are there days we want to scream? Yes. Do we look for answers and not always find them? Yes. We take what we've been given and try to make the best of it. We pray a lot, too."

Pam and Lind were fortunate that, unlike a lot of people who must cope with catastrophic illnesses, they had good health insurance. Still, it didn't cover everything. There were deductibles to be paid and many expenses that weren't covered. They paid $5000 for a wheelchair for Bobby, and later when it was rebuilt for Eric it wound up costing close to $15,000. They couldn't have afforded Eric's trip to Disney World, or Bobby's to Washington, if the Special Wish Foundation hadn't been there to help.

It was for people like the Krenzkes that Ramona Fickle founded A Special Wish. Today, A Special Wish has grown to twenty-one chapters, twenty in this country and one in Moscow. A Special Wish is not the only or even the largest wish-granting organization in the United States. The Make a Wish Foundation is the largest and there are several others. They all deserve our praise and support, but Ramona is proud that A Special Wish is the one that covers the largest time span in children's lives: it grants wishes from birth through age nineteen.

The wishes take many forms. The first wish granted, back in 1982, was to a six-year-old girl with cancer who wanted to go to Disney World. A boy of seventeen, with an incurable form of leukemia, wanted to meet golfer Payne Stewart, and after he did Stewart gave him the trophy he won in the 1993 Pro-Am tournament. When a ten-year-old boy with a rare form of cancer wanted a telescope, volunteers at Ohio State University's observatory bought him one and taught him to use it. The mother of a dying two-month-old child was given a special, adjustable chair that let her sleep with her baby in her arms.

The average cost of granting a wish is $2800. Ramona is proud that almost everyone who works for the foundation is a volunteer, that the foundation never uses professional fund raisers or solicits by phone, and the majority of their funds come from individual contributions.

A Special Wish and the other wish-granting organizations bring happiness to thousands of children who bear a terrible burden, and to their families, and they have changed many lives. They changed mine when they introduced me to the Krenzkes. I loved those boys. They were so different in their personalities: Bobby, the elder statesman, and Eric, the firecracker. Yet they shared the same open heart and dazzling smile, the same wanderlust eyes that glowed with lionlike fearlessness. I will never forget them. If I think about them hard, I cry at their loss. When I see two bright stars twinkling side by side on an impossibly clear night, I see Bobby and Eric.

The Happy
Helpers

Amber Coffman

"What can one person do?" I hear people ask. "The problems of society are so vast!" The answer is that one person can do a lot. Every great movement starts with one person and moves forward because of individuals. Today, as we confront homelessness in America, it's easy to say, "There's nothing I can do." In fact, a great many people are doing something to help the homeless, in churches and volunteer programs all across the land. One of these heroes is a fifteen-year-old girl I met in a small town in Maryland.

WHEN MOTHER TERESA came to Washington early in June 1997 to receive a gold medal from Congress, Speaker Newt Gingrich invited several colleagues to his office to meet her. Impatiently, we went out to the hallway and waited for her with a group of nuns. All of us, politicians and nuns alike, stood in reverent silence. When the elevator door opened, a small, seemingly fragile woman exited by wheelchair, smiling and lifting her hand to her lips in a prayerful act of humility. Back in Newt's office, Senators and Representatives lined up to greet her; Mother Teresa's love, humility and inner strength filled the room.

For decades, her spiritual energy reached out to countless lives, all around the world. On a visit to Glen Burnie, Maryland, a few weeks after I met Mother Teresa in Washington, I saw a dramatic example of the impact she had on the lives of others.

I had driven to Glen Burnie to meet fifteen-year-old Amber Coffman. Two months earlier, at the President's Summit for America's Future, in Philadelphia, I had heard that Amber had done a remarkable job of feeding the homeless and I wanted to see for myself.

Amber's mother, Bobbi Coffman, a gentle woman in her thirties, met me in the parking lot in front of her small, drab apartment complex. It was clear that working families lived here, many of whom were probably struggling financially. Bobbi took me to meet Amber and her volunteers. Inside the apartment, almost filling the small living room, was a table surrounded by kids making bologna and cheese sandwiches. I knew immediately which one was Amber. A slender, pretty girl with long, dark hair, she had the quiet aura of a born leader.

Working with her around the table were boys and girls, white and black, ranging from tiny six-year-olds to strapping sixteen-year-olds. They wore sneakers, T-shirts, jeans and cutoffs like any group of American kids, but they were different. On a Saturday morning when they might have been sleeping or hanging out at the mall or playing soccer, they had gathered to help others. Amber calls her program Happy Helpers for the Homeless, and these young people, and others like them, have met in the Coffman living room every Saturday morning since February 1993 to serve the homeless people of Glen Burnie and Baltimore.

Bobbi and Amber's apartment is a part-time kitchen for serving hungry homeless people. The worn couch in the living room was stacked with hundreds of buns for the sandwiches. The cramped kitchen was filled with cartons of juice. Big yellow mustard jars were scattered around the dining room. The young volunteers filled the rest of the apartment with their energy and laughter as they slapped together sandwiches with assembly-line efficiency. Their innocence and generosity, as they carried out this labor of kindness and love, brought tears to my eyes. Too often, growing up hardens our hearts and blocks our "childlike" instincts to help others.

That afternoon, Amber and her mother told me how the Happy Helpers came to be. Mother and daughter are very close. Amber's father deserted Bobbi before Amber was born. Bobbi served in the army for fifteen years, as a teacher, rising to the rank of staff sergeant. But when the army wanted to send her to a hardship post, where she didn't think eight-year-old Amber would be happy, she resigned and moved to Glen Burnie. In the army, she hadn't had time for volunteer work, but in her new life she wanted to work "with the poorest of the poor."

Bobbi wanted to volunteer at Sarah's House, a homeless shelter located on the Fort Meade army base, but she would only volunteer if her daughter would go with her.

"I was hesitant," Amber recalls. "I didn't know what to expect. But once we got there I really liked it."

Amber looked after homeless children while their parents took training courses. Both the children and their parents told Amber their stories. "They broke her heart," Bobbi recalls. "Driving home, she would tell me about their lives and we would both cry."

A year later, Amber read four books on Mother Teresa for a book report. "I was inspired," she recalls. "I wanted to start my own programs, to provide meals to people who aren't in shelters. Mother Teresa had dedicated her life to others—I wanted to be like her."

"I told her it was a wonderful idea," Bobbi recalls. "But I told her we'd have to wait until I got another job and saved enough money for us to get started. That took a year. We started the program in February 1993."

Amber had just turned eleven.

It's not unusual for a girl that age to take someone like Mother Teresa for her hero. In fact, Bobbi recalled that, when Amber was only four, her preschool teacher sent home a report that said, "Amber is a leader, and everyone else wants to follow." What is unusual is for someone so young to have the determination, the imagination and the organizational skills to start a program that would reach out to thousands of people in need.

"I knew I couldn't put a roof over their heads," Amber says. "But I wanted to do what I could. I was sure other kids would volunteer if they had a chance. I knew from the first that I wanted to provide meals. And I knew that giving them food wasn't as important as giving them love."

Over the years, Amber had attracted a total of six hundred volunteers. When I met her in 1997, she had about forty "active" volunteers, and each Saturday morning about ten of them would come to the apartment and make six hundred sandwiches. That translates into six hundred slices of cheese, six hundred hamburger buns, and forty-two pounds of bologna, plus the soft drinks, pastries and hot chocolate they serve in the winter. (Sometimes they make peanut butter and jelly sandwiches, but that takes longer.) On Saturday afternoon they distribute sandwiches to the handful of homeless people in Glen Burnie, and on Sunday they drive to Baltimore and give the rest of the sandwiches, along with juice, doughnuts, clothes and blankets, and toiletries such as soap and toothpaste, to several hundred homeless people who line up outside City Hall.

Amber estimates that Happy Helpers for the Homeless has fed more than 25,000 people since 1993, and her work has attracted national attention. When she appeared on the CBS Morning News, people across the country wrote to say they wanted to start Happy Helpers programs in their cities, and several are now under way. Thus, in a mysterious and wonderful way, the spark of goodness has passed from Mother Teresa to Amber, and from her to others all across the land.

Bobbi and Amber's motivation is in large part religious. Scriptural quotations are posted on their refrigerator door. Every Sunday, before they drive to Baltimore to feed the poor, they attend early services at the Heritage

Church of God. Today Bobbi has two jobs, during the day as a licensed child care provider and as an employee at the Greenway Bowling Center at night. Bobbi gives all the credit for the Happy Helpers to Amber—"It's not me, it's her," she insists—but it is clear that she is the rock that enabled her remarkable daughter to flourish.

The volunteers are remarkable too. When I asked them why they were there, working for others when they could be out having fun, they made it clear that this *was* fun.

"It helps people—it makes me feel good," said Jeff Mentzer, a sixteen-year-old from Severna Park, Maryland.

Jesse Pittman, who's seven, said, "I jumped up and down when I heard about Amber's program. My mom said it was a little far away but she'd take me." Her mother, Karen Pittman, explained that they are Quakers and live on a farm near Davidsonville, a half hour's drive away. When Jesse was five, she said, she began noticing homeless people when they went to town. "She just saw them as people," Karen says of her daughter. "She asked why they were on the street. I told her they didn't have homes and we started making sandwiches for them whenever we were going to town. She would give them a sandwich and talk with them and they were so happy to have a child talk to them. Then we heard about Amber's program and she knew she had to participate."

Most of the kids said they'd read about the Happy Helpers in the newspaper and called Amber to volunteer. Who says that kids don't read?

Amber not only directs the weekend sandwich making and distribution, but during the week seeks out businesses and restaurants and grocery stores that will donate food and other necessities to the homeless. Increasingly she is a sought-after public speaker. She doesn't ask for a fee, but when people offer money, it goes to buy more cheese and bologna.

When Amber started the Happy Helpers, she made a list of the things she needed. First of all she needed sources of food. "I drove her to the stores," her mother recalls, "but I always waited in the car while she went in to ask for donations. I knew a child would reach them. She got a lot of yeses." Their apartment building is next door to a 7-Eleven, which lets them store their sandwiches overnight in its freezer.

One of their biggest donors is Glenn Kikuchi, who owns a McDonald's in nearby Millersville, Maryland. When Amber went to see him a few years ago, he quizzed her for an hour before he agreed to support her. Bobbi estimates that in 1996 he donated 48,000 slices of cheese and 24,000 hamburger rolls.

The National Center for Pastoral Leadership has raised several thousand dollars that is used to buy food and other necessities. Another family donates twelve pounds of cheese each week. When Amber was at the Philadelphia conference on volunteerism, officials from B.J.'s Wholesale Club sought her out and asked how they could help. Now they send several hundred doughnuts and sweet rolls each week.

At the outset, Amber and her mother talked to homeless people and found that they were most in need of food on weekends, so they decided to distribute sandwiches in Glen Burnie on Saturdays, then in Baltimore, where the need is much greater, on Sundays. Bobbi says they haven't missed a weekend in more than four years. To them, showing up with the sandwiches is a moral imperative—they know the people will be there, counting on them, and they won't let them down.

When they first started the Happy Helpers, they distributed the sandwiches in downtown Glen Burnie, until the homeless people asked them to come closer to the woods where many of them live. So they began meeting outside a public library where many of them spend part of their time. They did that for several years until one day a security guard told them they were loitering and they couldn't pass out sandwiches there anymore. Amber doesn't know why the library changed its policy. Fortunately, it didn't matter, because Bobbi and Amber just moved their operation next door to the Harundale Presbyterian Church.

The Saturday I was there, a father and son, Joe Knight Sr. and Jr., came by for sandwiches and fruit juice, as they do most Saturdays. Both were down on their luck. The father said he receives Social Security and is living in a shelter while he waits to get into public housing. His son, a dark-haired man with a ponytail, said he had worked for many years as a furniture mover but now has a bad back and has been waiting for six months for his Social Security benefits to begin. Both men spoke affectionately of Amber and her mother: "They do a wonderful job," the father said. "We really look forward to seeing them every Saturday."

Amber insists that homeless people "are just like everybody else, just like you and me. A lot of them work. Some just have lost their jobs or had bad luck. We try to help them with their self-esteem." Her mother adds that some of the people they work with have drug or alcohol problems. Amber recalls one man who said that he would have starved without her help, but later found a job and got his life back together.

In addition to the weekend sandwich distribution, Amber holds a series of special events each year. On her birthday, instead of having a party for herself she gives a party for the homeless. Last Easter she and her volunteers gave out three hundred Easter baskets. Last Christmas she persuaded schools, churches and businesses to donate 1300 gifts for the homeless, which she and her friends wrapped and distributed. In October, on National Make a Difference Day, the Happy Helpers bring busloads of Baltimore's homeless to spend a day with Glen Burnie's homeless. The volunteers serve breakfast and lunch, wash the homeless people's clothes, have a barber to cut hair and a dentist who pulls teeth on the spot. Whenever they can, they give the homeless sneakers, wristwatches and sleeping bags.

"We have the largest family in the world," Amber says. She has plans to start a mentoring program, in which older teenagers and adults will work with homeless and at-risk children, with an emphasis on "homework and love."

Amber has begun to think about her future. When we met, she was a sophomore at Severn College Preparatory School. Although her grades are only average—she doesn't always have time to focus on her homework—I suspect that any college in America would love to have her a few years from now. After college, she has two goals.

The first is to create her own, family-oriented homeless shelter, where she and her mother would live with about ten people at a time. The other dream is to be a broadcast journalist.

Amber Coffman, as her preschool teacher realized, has a gift for leadership—leadership and love. To meet Amber and her friends is to have one's faith in America's youth restored. Too often, we only hear about the kids who go wrong. When good kids do good works it's just not news. But these young people—and there are tens of thousands like them, all over America—have the idealism and dedication to make a difference in a world that often their elders have made a mess of. They are without guile or cynicism. Amber and her friends haven't just shaken their heads and said how terrible social problems are— they have acted. They have done everything they can to help those in need. Just as Mother Teresa inspired Amber, Amber and her mother and her friends should be an inspiration to us all.

The Best Medicine

Michael Christensen

What is more terrible than the suffering of a child? And what is nobler than to relieve that suffering? Our nation has the finest medical care and technology in the world, yet suffering persists. But a clown named Michael Christensen came up with an idea that has helped ease the pain of thousands of boys and girls. His "wonder drug" was one that the experts had neglected: the gift of laughter.

I N 1990, *Life* magazine published a brilliant article, written by Brad Darrach, about Michael Christensen, the cofounder of the Big Apple Circus and founder of its Clown Care Unit. Here is how the writer summed up Michael's early life:

"Behind the comical false face lives a man who learned about laughter in the school of pain. Conceived out of wedlock, Michael Christensen was raised on the shabby side of Walla Walla, Washington, by an alcoholic mother who survived on welfare, ran through four husbands and died at 55. Bewildered and angry, the boy grew up believing he had 'no right to be here.' His idol was his older brother Kenneth. But at 14 Kenneth ran off to live with his father. Feeling abandoned and bitter, ten-year-old Michael began to shoplift and break into automobiles. Luckily, a juvenile court judge scared him back to the straight and narrow, and when he entered the University of Washington he discovered theater. In the late '70s he toured Europe as a street clown, then helped his friend Paul Binder create the Big Apple Circus. But the old trauma of abandonment lay buried in Michael's heart like a land mine waiting to explode."

The explosion came when Kenneth died of pancreatic cancer in 1985. By then, the Big Apple Circus was a success and Michael, as its creative director, had fame and fortune far beyond anything he had ever imagined. He had a happy marriage, too, and two young daughters, but none of that mattered. His brother's death sent him into a black hole of grief. Perhaps only those who have experienced great personal loss can understand the totality of that despair. It is then that you discover your core.

"All of us go through our own therapy," Michael says. "Even before my brother died, as I began to get healthy and to love myself the right way, I felt an urge to serve. The loss of my brother accelerated my commitment. When you suffer a loss like that, grief comes over you in waves, one after another. One night I went to the Episcopal church where I'm a member, in Pennsylvania. No one else was there and I allowed myself to be totally lost. I got on my knees and asked, 'What do You want me to do?' It was from that place that I made a commitment: any way I can be of service, I will. It was totally unconditional. When you do something like that, you are going to be taken up on your offer. It is not a logical process. I gave my life to something bigger than myself, to be used in whatever way. I didn't know what it would bring but I was ready for anything."

But how was he to serve? As Mr. Stubs, the beloved star clown of a great circus, he already brought laughter to hundreds of thousands of people each year. But he sought something more. It was then that Jenny Kein, the director of development at the Babies and Children's Hospital of New York, at Columbia-Presbyterian Medical Center, happened to call.

"Her first words were, 'Michael, I've been secretly in love with you for years—and now I have a favor to ask!' Then she told me about Heart Day, the reunion they have every two years for children who have been heart patients, and asked if I would perform. What could I say?"

Things had begun to come together. Shortly before

Michael's brother died, Michael and his family had gone to Seattle and spent a final week with him. During that week, Michael's brother gave him a doctor's black bag that he'd bought at a flea market. Every clown needed a doctor's bag, he said. "I took the bag home and put it on my shelf and it sat there for three months," Michael says.

In preparation for Heart Day, Michael toured the Babies and Children's Hospital—in street clothes—to gain a better understanding of the children and the hospital world. Then he and two of his colleagues adapted their clown routine to be a hospital routine. Mr. Stubs was reborn as Dr. Stubs. At the Heart Day ceremony, Michael waited in the wings while the master of ceremonies introduced the famous Dr. Stubs who was about to speak. Everyone in the audience thought a "real" doctor was about to appear.

"Then I walked onstage, carrying my black bag, and the kids went crazy," Michael recalls. "What followed was twenty minutes of the most fulfilling work I'd ever done. That was the beginning of Clown Care." That performance caused Michael to look beyond the fortunate children who attended the Big Apple Circus to the unfortunate children who were sick and dying in countless hospitals. His mission was clear. "I knew I was meant to help kids recover from the pain and fear of illness. It came out of an unconscious place in myself. After the grief of my brother's death, the creation of the Clown Care Unit gave me feelings of celebration and joy. Call it love and caring, God, a higher consciousness—whatever—I wanted to give my life to that."

Today, the Clown Care Unit has fifty-two clowns working in ten hospitals: seven in New York City, plus the Children's Medical Center in Washington, D.C., the Yale

New Haven Children's Hospital, and the nation's largest pediatric medical center, Boston's Children's Hospital.

The clowns work in pairs, moving about the wards in close harmony with the doctors and nurses, who have come to love them as much as the children. Indeed, the chief of pediatrics at one New York hospital said, "How stupid we were! Until the clowns came it never occurred to us that children who were desperately ill needed *fun!*"

One day Michael, as Dr. Stubs, let me accompany him and his colleagues, Dr. Comfort and Dr. Bones, as they made their rounds at Mount Sinai Medical Center on New York's Upper East Side. Michael was in his classic costume: painted-on black beard, big nose, battered fedora—and white doctor's smock. He explained that, for hospital rounds, the clowns don't paint themselves as boldly, and perhaps frighteningly, as they would for an arena performance. This is Clown Care, not Clown Scare, he explained.

I learned some other rules. We washed our hands thoroughly before we started our rounds. And we would never enter a child's room without his or her permission. Children in hospitals are powerless, he explained, at the mercy of people and forces beyond their control. The clowns empower them by asking permission to come into their lives.

The clowns create a caricature world of medicine. They play doctor, nurse or patient to touch the hearts and funny bones of children with little other laughter in their lives. Great clowns are like the distorting mirrors in sideshows. They study us shrewdly, then give us back an exaggerated version of ourselves that makes us laugh at our own foibles. Michael's clowns come complete with stethoscopes, white coats, and the mannerisms of the hospital community we have known in real life—or on "ER" and "Chicago Hope." Sometimes they move about solemnly, speaking in low, self-important tones that playfully mock doctors we all have known.

Dr. Stubs, Dr. Comfort and Dr. Bones started that morning's rounds in the Communicative Disease and Oncology ward. They quickly engaged a young patient in a slapstick routine. As they dropped their hats, their plastic "medical tools"—saw, hammers, crowbars—the girl brightened, and she was belly-laughing when they moved on.

Next, at the bedside of a teenage boy, they improvised a makeshift band. A stethoscope became a horn, a hypodermic was transformed into a flute, and they arranged for the young patient to provide the "pop" in "Pop Goes the Weasel."

Later they moved among three- and four-year-olds who had undergone painful treatments for cancer. Children's immediate reaction to tall people in white coats is fear and anger. Even those with red noses and baggy pants are threatening until they prove themselves friendly. Michael and his colleagues were gentle and loving as they worked to coax a smile from these vulnerable children. Dr. Comfort quietly manipulated a hand puppet for nearly ten minutes to reach one boy, talking to him all the while in a soft and loving voice. Suddenly, the sun broke through: the boy smiled and the adults looking on applauded. Some of their parents, watching, found their eyes glistening with tears.

Dr. Stubs blew huge bubbles to get one girl's attention. Her wheelchair hummed with beeps and buzzes from the equipment that regulated her IV. The third bubble was the charm: she reached out to it with tiny hands and then was caught up in the game. Michael blew bubbles furiously and soon transported the child and her mother to a better reality, at least for a while.

Sometimes clowning is just old-fashioned slapstick. One member of Clown Care, Dr. Know Nothing (Jonah Emsig in real life), rarely passes through a door without first banging into it several times. Sometimes they touch us with acts of tenderness that carry us back to our youth. For example, Dr. E-B-D-B-D (Laine Barton, who holds a master's degree in psychology but prefers being a clown) can bring tears to your eyes by playing her ukulele and singing "Dream a Little Dream of Me." Then, minutes later, she brings laughter with her comic rendition of a hillbilly ditty that goes, "I got tears in my ears from crying over you."

The clowns love their work, yet they talk, too, about the "emotional hygiene" meetings they and other clowns have each month. It isn't easy dealing with dying children and their parents day after day. They talk about the boundaries they must set on how emotionally involved they will let themselves become. "It's been harder since I've had a child of my own," Laine Barton says.

Paul Cothran, the unit's director of health and community services, often is brought to tears by reading the letters that families write to Clown Care. Those whose children have returned home write to thank the clowns for making their hospital stay so much brighter. Others, whose children have died, write to thank them for bringing joy to their final days.

Michael believes there is a kind of divine mystery about the way the circus and the Clown Care Unit have unfolded. They haven't planned things, he says, so much as they have just happened. "What we have needed always comes to us," he says. The 1990 *Life* magazine story was an example. No press agent sold *Life* on that story, which was the most publicity the program had ever received. The unit's manager was having a massage one day, and talking about his work, when the woman giving him the massage said, "My husband is a writer for *Life* magazine—I'll bet he'd be interested in that."

The *Life* article focused on a heartrending case in which Michael set no boundaries on his love for a Puerto Rican boy named Carmelo who has spent most of his life in hospitals. His kidneys collapsed when he was three. At six he had a stroke. At eight he developed a serious heart condition. By the age of fourteen he was no bigger than a child of five. Yet he burned with a rage to live, and he tongue-lashed doctors and nurses, demanding their attention and respect.

"Get out of here!" the boy cried the first time Dr. Stubs came to his door. For two months, Michael came to Carmelo's bedside, singing songs, blowing bubbles, only to be ignored or told to go away. But, remembering his own unhappy childhood, Michael would not give up, and finally he won the boy over. At that point, Carmelo became an honorary clown and Michael would wheel him around the hospital and let him help entertain the other children.

In time, Carmelo was well enough to leave the hospital, but he had no place to go. Michael told his wife, Karyn, that he wanted to adopt the boy. Karyn wasn't sure. Even if Medicare would pay Carmelo's medical expenses, he would need twenty-four-hour-care, and the Christensens already had two young daughters. The issue became moot when Carmelo's father returned, with a new girlfriend who was determined to be Carmelo's mother.

Carmelo died just before the *Life* article appeared. Brad Darrach later told Michael it was his favorite of all the articles he'd written in a long career. When Darrach himself died in 1997, his family asked that, instead of flowers, donations be made to the Clown Care Unit.

Clown Care has brought happiness to thousands of

young people who urgently needed laughter in their lives. Such a good idea is inevitably spreading. In addition to the ten existing units, Clown Care is talking to hospitals in Los Angeles, Seattle, Philadelphia and Chicago. The challenge is to ensure that each unit is professionally trained and solidly financed. Paul Cothran estimates that each unit costs about $250,000 a year, primarily for the clowns' salaries, and he says the host hospital usually raises about half that, with the other half coming from donations and foundations. (I first heard of Clown Care from officials at the Pfizer Foundation, which supports it and many other worthwhile programs.) The money has always turned up. Clown Care is too good an idea to stop.

When I said goodbye to Michael outside an elevator in the crowded Mount Sinai Hospital, I felt both joy and sadness. Many people suffer but few are privileged to bring such beauty out of their suffering. In parting, I hugged my new friend. "God bless you!" I told him. We have all been blessed by what this good man has given us through Clown Care.

A Lump
in the Throat

Dr. Jack McConnell

It was a hot, bright August afternoon when I got off the bus that had carried me from the Savannah airport to Hilton Head Island, South Carolina. A tall, slender gentleman waved and came toward me with hand outstretched. I liked Dr. Jack Mc-Connell at once—the twinkle in his eye, his brisk step, his kind heart, his sense of fun were all plain to see. He was soft-spoken and modest, yet I could tell he was reinforced with steel. Thanks to his vision, compassion and determination, 10,000 people have access to medical care who didn't have it before. And if he has his way, many thousands more, all over America, will also have free care.

I N JUNE 1989, at the age of sixty-four, Jack McConnell decided to retire after a distinguished career in medical research. In nearly thirty years with Johnson & Johnson, he guided the development of both Tylenol tablets and the Tine test, which is used in the diagnosis of tuberculosis, and carried out pioneering studies in human gene research. The son of a West Virginia minister, Jack McConnell had achieved rags-to-riches success and virtually every honor that American medicine can bestow.

After living many years in New Jersey, Dr. McConnell and his wife Mary Ellen chose Hilton Head Island, South Carolina, for their retirement home. Hilton Head, first developed in the 1960s, is a beautiful, slightly unreal world of expensive homes, marinas and cabin cruisers, world-class golf courses, and elegant shops and restaurants. Not surprisingly, many well-to-do people retire there. Jack McConnell loves, among other things, golf, jazz, good wine and camping trips with his wife and children, and he thought Hilton Head would be an excellent base for a vigorous retirement.

The something unexpected happened. Jack McConnell found himself bored with retirement.

After that, a chance encounter changed his life and many other lives as well.

"Robert Frost said that every poem starts with a lump in the throat," he told me. "Something like that led to Volunteers in Medicine. One night we had a heavy storm. The next morning it was still raining as I went for a drive outside Hilton Head's back gate. I passed a man who was wearing a wool coat and walking with a purposeful step. I stopped and offered him a ride, as I often do.

" 'Where are you headed?' I asked.

" 'I'm looking for a job.'

" 'What do you do?'

" 'Construction work.'

"I knew of a construction site nearby, and I offered to drive him there. On the way, I asked him what kind of health insurance he had. He said he didn't have any. He went on to tell me that, while his health was good, his wife suffered from a bad heart, diabetes and failing eyesight, all of which mostly went untreated. I thought, 'How can this be? How can we let this happen?'

"When we reached the construction site, I introduced him to the foreman, who established that he was a skilled worker and hired him on the spot. I started to leave, but the man took my arm and turned me around and gave me a hug. I was stunned. I was able to help that man, but why couldn't we help others like him?"

Jack McConnell thought a lot about that man, and the more he thought the more his conscience bothered him. He realized that when you left the privileged enclave of Hilton Head you stepped into another world, where many people lacked health insurance or decent medical care. Yet there on Hilton Head Island, he knew, were scores of doctors—and nurses, dentists and other professionals—who, like himself, were bored with golf, tennis, bridge and the other supposed joys of retirement.

In January 1992 he called a meeting at the Hilton Head Hospital. He described his vision: retired doctors and other professionals would be the volunteer staff of a new, free clinic that would serve those in and near Hilton Head who lacked health insurance and adequate health care.

Sixteen physicians said they would volunteer in the clinic if Dr. McConnell could make it happen. Encouraged, Jack started work on several fronts. He had to raise the money to build the clinic and he faced political and bureaucratic challenges as well.

You might think that no one would oppose a free clinic to help the poor—but you would be wrong. There were many who questioned it. Some doctors saw a free clinic as unwanted competition. ("How many of these patients who can't pay anything do you want?" Jack demanded of some local doctors who opposed him.) Some trial lawyers feared they wouldn't be able to sue it. And some bureaucrats just naturally oppose any new idea.

"All the physicians asked for two things," Dr. Mc-Connell says. "First, that they not have their life savings put at risk by malpractice suits as a result of volunteering. Second, they didn't want to pay a thousand dollars and take an eight-hour test to prove they were doctors."

Jack went before the South Carolina Board of Medical Licensure, seeking to have the testing and fees waived for his volunteer doctors who had practiced in other states. He found that the board members—average age about seventy-five—were highly skeptical.

"We have to treat everyone the same," the chairman told him.

"We have ten thousand people who aren't being treated at all," Jack declared.

"You're twisting my words against me," the chairman complained.

When Jack persisted, he was shown the door. He left thinking his project might be going down in flames, but he took his case to the state legislature, where he received a friendlier hearing. Legislation was passed to waive fees and testing for volunteers in his clinic, and the legislature also agreed that the state's Good Samaritan law, which placed a cap of $200,000 on malpractice awards given as a result of free care by a doctor in an emergency, could also apply to free care at the new clinic.

By February 1993, fifty-five physicians, sixty-eight nurses, seven dentists, two chiropractors, eight social workers, two dental assistants, two medical technicians, and more than a hundred lay persons had volunteered. The town of Hilton Head had agreed to lease Volunteers in Medicine a one-acre building site for the clinic for a dollar a year. Virtually all the clinic's equipment was donated. The money was raised, mostly in the Hilton Head community, and with no government money.

By the summer of 1993, operating out of temporary space at the Hilton Head Hospital, VIM began a program of free immunizations. The new clinic opened its doors in July 1994. When I visited there in the summer of 1997, it was treating about a thousand patients each month—and fourteen of his original sixteen volunteer doctors were still hard at work.

Jack told me that one of the clinic's first patients was the wife of the man he had picked up on the road that rainy morning several years before—the construction worker whose plight had inspired the clinic. The woman was treated for her problems with diabetes, her heart and her eyesight. One day Dr. McConnell saw her at the clinic and asked how she was doing. "I've found heaven," she told him. "I've cried away all my tears and there's nothing left but laughter."

The Volunteers in Medicine clinic is an attractive, inviting place. Just inside the front door is a playroom for children that is filled with books and toys. "We have just one rule," Dr. McConnell explains. "If a child reads a book, he or she has to take it home."

From the first, Dr. McConnell was determined to create a "culture of caring," where those who came for help would be seen not as "patients" but as friends and neighbors who happened to be in need. Greeters are on hand to welcome all new arrivals to the clinic and make them feel welcome. If they must wait to see a doctor, it is in a "reception area," not a "waiting room." Patients are told, often to their amazement, that there are no charges, no bills, no insurance forms to fill out. The free clinic really is free.

Because of the volunteer talent available in Hilton Head, the clinic offers a level of service that any city in America would be glad to claim. Services provided include vaccinations, physical exams, adult medicine, minor surgery, neurology, dermatology, postnatal and well-baby care, cardiology, pediatric care, eye and ear services, dental care, a pharmacy, gynecology and mental health and social services. The clinic addresses not only illnesses but the lifestyle choices that cause up to three quarters of all medical problems. There are classes not only on literacy but on such things as diet, diabetes, hypertension and CPR.

To qualify for service, an individual must live or work on Hilton Head Island or nearby Daufuskie Island, must have an income of no more than twice the official poverty level (about $29,000 for a family of four), and must either have no health insurance or be significantly underinsured. Dr. McConnell says these rules give VIM a target population of about ten thousand people, some of them the uninsured employees of Hilton Head's luxury hotels, shops and restaurants. This target population is about forty-five percent white, forty-five percent black, and ten percent Hispanic. Recently, All Saints Episcopal Church organized a

Friends on Wheels program, in which volunteers provide transportation to and from the clinic for those who need it. For all the early concern about liability insurance, so far the clinic has never faced a malpractice suit and doesn't expect to.

Most of the volunteer doctors and nurses come in one day a week, although some work more. Five paid employees oversee the volunteers. The clinic has weekly lectures and training programs to make sure the staff stays up to date professionally, and there is intensive peer review. Dr. McConnell and others at the clinic say staff morale could not be higher. "Our doctors have been freed from the need to earn money," McConnell says. "What they did need was to practice their profession and serve others in a hassle-free environment. This is a win-win situation that costs nothing—just give of yourself. It's one of the most beautiful and enriching things we can do."

I spoke with the clinic's oldest volunteer, a wonderful gentleman named Art Friedman. Art is a handsome, compact, white-haired eighty-seven-year-old doctor who practiced for many years in Youngstown, Ohio, then for ten years in San Diego before he and his wife retired to Hilton Head in 1991. Tragically, his wife died soon after they arrived. He survived his sorrow by becoming one of VIM's first volunteers, and one of the few who comes in five days a week.

"I'm Jewish," Dr. Friedman told me, "and one of the principles of Judaism is to help people. It's a spiritual and moral obligation. Of those to whom much is given, much is expected. It makes me feel good when I help people. Medicine was good to me and I want to give something back. Frankly, I don't know what I'd have done without this clinic. I had a girlfriend for fifty-five years and when I lost her I was really lost. We were hoping for sixty years but God settled us for fifty-five. We lived in California for ten years. We had a very social life, but when my wife became sick our social friends vanished like butterflies in the wind. I can count on people here in Hilton Head. The atmosphere at the clinic is wonderful. There is no competition here. Everyone is out to help the next fellow. Every doctor is a consultant to the other doctors."

I asked Dr. Friedman how he liked working for nothing.

He laughed and replied, "I make a million dollars every day. What I get from this clinic you can't buy with money."

Jack McConnell, who turned Volunteers in Medicine from a dream to a reality, is a tall, slender, modest man with thinning hair and skin well tanned by the South Carolina sun. When I asked him to explain his motivation, he was quick to say it was the religious faith he learned as a child in West Virginia.

"My faith is the strongest element in my life," he told me. "It's basic to my marriage and my work ethic. Love is what this program is all about. Until every American is healthy and whole, none of us is healthy and whole. Until all of us have peace, none of us has peace."

He says of his boyhood: "My parents were born in log cabins that their parents built. I grew up in the last house in the hollow in a coal mining community in Crumpler, West Virginia. I'm the son of a parsonage. My father was a Methodist minister who never earned more than $150 a month in his life. I grew up with the example my parents set. In the Depression, we often served lunch to forty or fifty people. Someone had put a mark on our front gate and people who were riding the rails knew that if they stopped in our town we would feed them. We didn't have much, but we had a big garden and they could pick corn and tomatoes and we would find a chicken somewhere and make a meal for everyone."

Despite a lack of money, Dr. McConnell told me, he and his six siblings have seven B.A. degrees and several graduate degrees among them. All the others became teachers. The way they got through college, he explained, was that his father provided the money to help the oldest sister through the first two years of college, then the father and the oldest sister helped the next one, and it went on like that, right down the line, until every brother and sister had a degree. Caring and sharing were the most basic part of the heritage Jack took away from his home in West Virginia.

Jack got his undergraduate degree at the University of Virginia, then his medical degree at the University of Tennessee. He was trained as a pediatrician, served for a time as a doctor in Africa, and joined Johnson & Johnson because he loved the intellectual challenge of medical research. For all Jack's success and honors as a scientist, he says the Volunteers in Medicine clinic means more to him that anything he's done—except for his marriage and family. Mary Ellen is busy with church work and, of their three children, Steve is a computer specialist, Kate is a massage therapist, and Page, perhaps inspired by his father's love of music, is the keyboardist with the popular rock group Phish.

Jack McConnell is proud of the clinic's success, but even prouder that other communities around the country are studying its example and starting free clinics that draw on retired doctors and nurses. He says that nine clinics are under way in such places as Newark, New Jersey, Erie, Pennsylvania, Wooster, Ohio, East St. Louis, Missouri, Stuart, Florida, and Columbus, Indiana. He says that each clinic is different. Few communities have a pool of retired medical talent equal to that in Hilton Head, but they draw upon their own resources. For example, some are closely tied to churches or to local hospitals. Dr. McConnell now spends much of his time working with the Volunteers in Medicine Clinic Institute, which is helping other communities start their own free clinics. Several hundred communities have expressed interest, he says, and he is writing a start-up curriculum to speed them on their way.

Jack McConnell is a wise and determined man who has looked at our society, seen one of its most glaring needs and done something about it. He points out that there are 170,000 retired doctors in America, and that if even half of them would volunteer, part time, they could provide primary care for most of the forty million people in America who don't have it. As he sees it, America does not have a health-care crisis, it has a crisis of values and vision.

"The hallmark of our society is the speed of change," he told me. "The ground is shifting under our feet. As we increase individual longevity, how do we organize our new society? How do retired people have more fulfilled lives? Our clinic brought two problems together and found a solution. I never had to recruit anyone. I just provided an opportunity for service and people came to it. Now we have physicians who retire to Hilton Head specifically because the clinic is here. It provides an outlet for the reservoir of good will people have for others in need. Give people a spot where they can help and they'll come running. It's citizens helping other citizens, and that is citizenship at its best. We have to do more of this. America can be better and more compassionate without anyone losing, and with everyone gaining. People can augment the government and government can support the people."

As Dr. McConnell sees it, his clinic, and others like it, can be significant agents of change: "They can transform the lives of friends and neighbors, the lives of the volunteers, and by extension transform a town into a community. No town can become a community as long as we leave behind a segment of the population in need of the basics of life."

When I asked this good and wise man to sum up his philosophy, he simply recited VIM's mission statement:

MAY WE HAVE EYES TO SEE THOSE WHO ARE
INVISIBLE AND EXCLUDED

OPEN ARMS AND HEARTS TO REACH OUT
AND INCLUDE THEM

HEALING HANDS TO TOUCH THEIR LIVES
WITH LOVE

AND IN THE PROCESS HEAL OURSELVES

For Jack McConnell, those are not just high-minded words. He has the courage to live by them. His example shines like a beacon to others who want to serve. When we parted, I thought that, if guardian angels exist, this man is my idea of what one should be: kind, fun, firm, creative and inspiring.

You Don't Know How Much I Hate Drugs

Jessica Hulsey

I met Hope the other day. Her name was Jessica Hulsey and her early years were a nightmare of poverty, drug addiction and the terrible helplessness of a child adrift in a world she can neither control nor understand. Yet Jessica had the courage to overcome adversity and build a new life. Today, twenty-one and a graduate of a major university, she is determined to help others avoid the drug abuse that so devastated her own family. Jessica's full story still lies ahead of her, but it is already remarkable.

THE FIRST THING you notice about Jessica Hulsey is her physical beauty: at twenty-one, she is tall and slender, with a lovely smile, long brown hair and dark, watchful eyes. As she speaks, you realize that she is also poised, articulate and intelligent. Then, as you grasp her story of growing up with two heroin-addicted parents, you realize that Jessica has lived through a hell that most of us cannot imagine and come out of it strong and wise and determined to share her antidrug message with all America.

I first heard Jessica speak at the President's Summit for America's Future in Philadelphia in April 1997. Like everyone else in the huge audience, I was transfixed by her account of a childhood on the streets of Long Beach, California, with addicts for parents. Hungry and dirty, struggling to survive and care for her younger sister, she somehow took control of her life and eventually escaped to Princeton University.

Jessica is very open about what she lived through. She has told her story many times, to audiences all over America. The memories are painful, but she feels that being honest about her childhood helped her survive and now can help others as well. By contrast, she thinks that both her mother and her younger sister internalized their anger and pain and that worsened their problems. The one thing Jessica asked, as she told me her story, was that I not dwell exclusively on the sensational parts of her life, as some journalists have, because she thinks what is important is that she survived and is helping others avoid the tragedy of drug abuse. Nonetheless, only by understanding what she has been through can we fully understand the truth of her message.

The best place to start Jessica's story is with her grandmother, Zoe Breaux, a full-blooded Chippewa Indian who grew up in Michigan. Zoe went to California and married a man whom Jessica describes as a "nasty, abusive alcoholic" who mistreated his wife and daughters. Zoe, who is a strong woman, divorced the man when Jessica's mother, Annette, was ten, but damage had been done.

"My mom began using drugs the same way most kids do," Jessica says. "She started with alcohol and marijuana when she was thirteen. By fifteen it was LSD and by sixteen it was cocaine. One drug led to another, which is something a lot of kids don't understand. Her mother and stepfather threw her out of the house when she was fifteen and she began to live on the street. She met my father, Terry, who was several years older and already addicted to heroin. She married him when she was eighteen. I was born when she was nineteen and after that she started using heroin. She was addicted by the time my sister was born, when I was three."

Jessica has vivid memories of those early years. The family lived on the streets, in parked cars, in seedy motels. The first word her sister could spell was "motel." She saw her parents and their friends shooting up with heroin. At age four or five, she shocked her grandmother with a graphic description of how you cook the heroin in a spoon and fill the syringe. From the first, she felt protective toward her sister, Terri Lynn, as if she was her mother. The girls' only refuge came when Annette would drop them off to spend time with their grandmother and her second husband at their home in Buena Park. In those days, Zoe would buy her and Terri Lynn toys and clothes, but Annette would take the gifts back to the store and demand the money back so she could use it to buy heroin.

Jessica says both her parents are brilliant people, although neither graduated from high school. Her father has mechanical skills—he can fix anything, Jessica says—and worked as a TV repairman to feed his addiction. Jessica says her father urged her mother to resort to other, illegal means of earning money for drugs.

When Jessica was four, her mother was jailed on a forgery charge—she thinks she took the blame for something Terry had done—and Jessica and her sister went to live full time with their grandmother. The move was heaven for the two girls. "We had our own rooms and blue bed sheets and plenty to eat and clean clothes. We went to school and to church. They took us on trips. We were so glad to have plenty to eat and a roof over our heads."

Zoe took the girls to visit their mother in jail and later, when Annette was freed, the sisters sometimes spent weekends with her, but they continued to live with their grandmother. This paradise crumbled when Jessica was eight and her mother insisted that the girls return to live with her. Jessica's grandparents felt they had no legal grounds to resist, so they reluctantly turned the sisters back over to their mother. By then Annette had divorced Terry and married another addict. Back with their mother, the girls' lives were once again chaos; they had no real home and not enough to eat. They would be left for hours in a parked car or with a drug dealer, a woman with children who doubled as a baby-sitter.

"We spent a lot of time pulling lice out of each other's hair," Jessica recalls. "My sister didn't go to school at all that year. I went half the year, then they made me leave because of the lice. But I made up the work and passed. Sometimes we'd be left in a car parked near where our father worked. There was an automobile junkyard nearby and that was our playground. For a while we lived in a kind of group house with about fourteen people who were all addicts, including some of my aunts and uncles."

After Annette's second husband was sent to prison for parole violations, she and her daughters often visited him on weekends at the Federal Correctional Institution at Terminal Island. Jessica spent much of her time in the prison library, where she could read and check books out. She was always an overachiever, determined to do her best. She never hid the facts of her life from her teachers. Zoe says that when Jessica was in kindergarten, and the students were supposed to talk about their families, Jessica wanted to talk about her parents' drug abuse, but the teacher persuaded her not to, lest the other children tease or torment her about it.

Throughout all this, Jessica's religion helped sustain her. "When I was very young, I read the Book of Job, over and over, because I believed that somehow I was being tested like Job and there was a reason for my life and I would come through it."

Several months after Annette had taken her daughters back, their father found them in a parked car where she had left them. He took them to Zoe, who sought the advice of a lawyer. At his urging, she called the police and had the girls put in protective custody, pending a court hearing on custody. The girls lived in a Los Angeles County foster care shelter for about ten days, until a court hearing awarded custody to Zoe and her husband.

"After that, they lived with us," Zoe says. "We didn't have much money but we tried to give them a normal life.

They had piano lessons and we took trips in the summers. They saw their mother on weekends. Their father had given up any claim to them."

The trauma of losing her daughters caused Annette to do something she had never done before: enter a rehabilitation program and stick with it. As a result in 1987, when Jessica was eleven, Annette brought suit to regain custody of her daughters.

"The custody fight was one of the worst things that happened to me," Jessica says. "I was in the sixth grade. The law favors the natural parent and I was terrified that I'd have to go back to my mother. They let me testify. I remember facing the two lawyers, with the judge beside me. My grandmother's lawyer asked, 'How does it feel when you go to spend weekends with your mother?'

"I said, 'It jeopardizes my home life and my sense of security,' and everybody laughed. But the judge let us stay with my grandmother."

Jessica is quick to add, "I don't blame my mother. The drugs took control of her life. She doesn't even remember much of her twenties—it's all a blur. I love her very much. I haven't suffered. What happened to her was much worse than what happened to me."

Jessica's parents were part of an extended family of drug abusers. "There's no one in my family except me who hasn't been an addict," she says.

Her father's brother broke into a house to get money for heroin and was shot by the owner and paralyzed from the waist down. Despite his disability he kept using heroin and died of an overdose at forty.

Her mother's sister's first husband lost his business because of drug abuse and began manufacturing methamphetamine, or speed. This led to a dispute with a gang whose members tied him up in a motel room and gave him a "hot shot"—an overdose of heroin—then threw him into a ditch to die. "He was my favorite uncle," she says. "He was like a father to me. He made mistakes but he didn't deserve to die like that."

Jessica can remember her father's younger sister as a beautiful young girl. But by her late twenties "heroin had destroyed her—she looked fifty."

Jessica's mother separated from her second husband but when he was dying of kidney failure and liver problems, brought on by drug abuse, she took him back and cared for him until he died.

Somehow, out of all this pain and devastation, Jessica learned a lesson of love. "Whether or not you do drugs has nothing to do with whether you're a good or bad person. Drugs can take over anyone's life. I love my family. I just don't understand why they do everything the hard way. I thank my mother. Because she was a drug addict, I never will be. She learned my lessons for me."

After the court granted permanent custody of Jessica and Terri Lynn to their grandmother, Jessica was able to concentrate on school and on her burning desire to overcome the life she had known. Looking back, she believes she has had many blessings, starting with the love and security her grandmother provided. She is also grateful to Lisa Myers, a woman in her twenties who was a Big Sister volunteer in a counseling program Jessica took part in. "She was the first woman I ever met who had gone to college. She would take me to movies and museums and poetry readings, and I got to know her family. She introduced me to possibilities I hadn't known existed. Knowing her made me want to go to college. Lisa wore glasses and I wanted so much to be like her that I tried to flunk an eye exam so I could wear glasses too."

When Jessica was fifteen, as a student at Cypress High

School, she read an anti-drug newsletter published by the Orange County sheriff's office. She called and volunteered to write for the newsletter, and in time told a deputy about her family's drug use. He invited her to speak at a dinner given by an anti-drug organization called Drug Use Is Life Abuse, or DUILA. By the time Jessica finished telling her story at the dinner, most of the audience was in tears. Jessica found that she liked talking about her experiences. It was a way to use her life to warn others about drugs. Soon she was on the board of directors of DUILA, and was vice-president of the Orange County Students Against Drug Abuse and president of Cypress High Against Drugs.

During her last two years of high school, Jessica spoke all over America. After she spoke to the national conference of the Community Anti-Drug Coalitions of America, she became chair of its student advisory committee and a member of its board of directors. She also wrote articles for the *Los Angeles Times* and spoke to the President's Drug Abuse Council in Washington.

She became close to DUILA's director, Julie Holt, whom she came to think of as her mentor. "She gave me confidence in my abilities and encouraged me to set my goals high. She encouraged me to go to college and helped me with my public speaking, job interviewing and stress management. Her care and concern helped bring me where I am today."

A Princeton graduate in the audience at one of her speeches arranged for another alumnus to interview her. Jessica had excelled in more than her anti-drug activities. She ran on the track team, was editor of her high school newspaper and president of the Ecology Club, wrote an essay that won her a Rotary Club trip to Japan, and was a National Merit Scholar. Still, for all her achievements, she had never imagined that she might attend an Ivy League college. To her amazement, she was offered a scholarship to Princeton.

To leave her mother and sister and grandmother, even for Princeton, was hard. The decision was made harder by the fact that her sister was starting to have the kinds of problems that Jessica had avoided. Always rebellious, Terri Lynn dropped out of school in the ninth grade, began using drugs and moved in with her mother. Jessica realized that, if she stayed in the Los Angeles area, a great deal of her time and energy would be consumed by her family and its problems. In a very real sense, Jessica had to save herself.

At first Jessica was intimidated by Princeton, but she soon fell in love with its beauty and the opportunity it gave her to read and think and learn. "I was afraid at first, not sure I could compete," she says, "but now I think I was meant to go to Princeton." During her first year she entered a relationship with a young man that still endures in their senior year and—she hopes—will continue after they graduate.

If Jessica had any complaint about Princeton, it was the drinking that went on there. "My first year I didn't want to go outside of my room, there was so much drinking," she says, only partly in jest. "I feel strongly that no one should drink until they're twenty-one. I hate to see people hurting themselves, acting stupid and making themselves sick. It's really boring being around a bunch of drunk people."

Jessica realizes that she can't go to parties and lecture everybody who's holding a beer, but she hopes to set an example. As president of her sorority, Kappa Alpha Theta, she has tried to be a role model for the younger girls. "I want them to see that I can be social and fun and not drink." After turning twenty-one, Jessica tried wine a few times, but she thinks she—or anyone—can have a better time without drinking. Moreover, she fears she may be pre-disposed to addiction and she sees no reason to take chances. Her vice is Coca-Cola. She downs several a day—too many, she admits—because the caffeine helps her stay awake to read or study.

Jessica chose to major in English at Princeton. Her love of literature has given her a private space that is all her own, a life apart from her continuing crusade against drugs. Yet she has also been a leader in volunteer and anti-drug activities. She is a project director with the Student Volunteer Council, which places students in a variety of programs. She works as a prevention coordinator at Corner House, a counseling center, which often sends her to speak to schools and community groups. She has been Outreach chair—in charge of recruiting volunteers—for her residential college, for the Episcopal church of Princeton and for her sorority. She has also recruited scores of students to serve as mentors to young people—remembering how much her mentors meant to her in her years of need. She is upset when students tell her they don't have time for volunteer work, because she believes they don't understand that volunteer work not only helps someone else, it helps you too.

Jessica often takes her anti-drug message to high school students. "I don't look or talk or dress different from them," she says. "I don't preach to them, I share. I have a long history of seeing drugs up close. You can't deny my authority. I try to challenge them. I tell them that when you're in high school and college you're setting a pattern for the rest of your life. If you go out and get drunk every night, you may do it forever. Why not say, 'Okay, maybe I'll drink once in a while, maybe I'll have wine with dinner sometimes, but not every night. I don't need chemicals to have a good time.'

"I tell them to take a stand. Don't do what the crowds do. They ask how, and I tell them I've done it. It isn't always easy not drinking in a society where drinking is very prevalent. I tell them, 'Forty percent of you could be predisposed to addiction, and we don't know which ones you are.'

"I think I hit home with a lot of kids. They come up afterward and say they identify with my message. I talk about dealing with anger, too. If you don't deal with it positively, it can destroy you. At one point, I got tired of telling my story. I don't want people only to see me for that. It gets hard. I wanted to move away from it. But I talked to a friend who said the point was more than my family. What I lived through is part of who I am and I think telling it can do good. My message isn't just drugs. We all have adversity in life and we have to learn to deal with it. My message is, you can overcome adversity and reach your goals."

Striding across the Princeton campus, Jessica is the picture of a happy, healthy, confident young woman, yet she has always felt a little apart from the other students, few of whom have known the kind of hardship she grew up with. She says it is always a shock to leave "my cozy life at Princeton" and return to the continuing chaos of her family.

"When I was a freshman at Princeton, I went home and saw my father for the first time in a long time, and it was shattering. He was living on the streets of Los Angeles. In addition to heroin, he now uses crack cocaine. The drugs have damaged not only his body but his mind. Last summer I went to see him. He lives with all these people. His sister lit a crack pipe in front of me. I was furious. Even my father said, 'Don't you know not to do that in front of Jessica?' He came to my twenty-first birthday party. It was funny—he ate so much, because he never eats. After the party, he asked if he could borrow money for cigarettes. There was no way I was going to give him money because I knew he'd spend it on drugs. So I went to a liquor store and bought him some cigarettes. I love my father but I have to accept that he is lost and I may never really know him."

Her sister Terri Lynn had a baby at seventeen. Since the baby arrived, Jessica says, she has stopped drugs and is getting her high school degree and seeking a job. Jessica's mother has been off drugs for more than a decade and the two of them have become very close. Unfortunately, Annette suffers from hepatitis C, a liver disease she probably contracted during her years of addiction.

As Jessica neared her graduation from Princeton, she gave a lot of thought to what she wants to do with her life. She believes that she survived her childhood for a reason: to warn others about the dangers of drugs. "All that I went through means nothing if I don't use it. That struggle made me who I am. There's nothing that means more to me than helping other people as I have been helped. I hate drugs. You have no idea how much I hate drugs. Even my closest friends can't begin to understand how much I hate drugs."

During her senior year at Princeton, Jessica hadn't decided how best to pursue her mission. She loves children and has thought of teaching, and she has also thought about studying to be an Episcopal priest. During college, Jessica spent two summers working as an intern for the Community Anti-Drug Coalition, in Alexandria, Virginia. Her duties included writing and research, and attending Congressional hearings, and she learned how exciting it can be to change policy through the political process.

Jessica hates the drugs but not the abusers. Although she opposes any legalization of drugs, she thinks treatment, not jail, is the answer for most drug abusers. If people must be jailed, she thinks, they must receive treatment there. She thinks more anti-drug education, starting at earlier ages, is needed in the schools. She warns students that marijuana is both addictive and a "gateway" to other drugs. She would like to see tougher laws against drunk driving. Based on her own life experience, she wants to see drug abuse treated more as a public health problem.

Jessica is someone who could literally do anything. She is steel inside. She told me of a party where a drunk student kept grabbing at her. "Finally, I slugged him," she says. "I may look fragile but I'm tough—I'm a street kid." She also clashed—verbally—with a famous television personality when she was a consultant to a special program on drugs. He thought she was overly opinionated for someone of her years; she thought he was pompous and naive.

At the time I talked with Jessica she was, like most college seniors, wondering what opportunities might come her way, what choices might be best for her. But I have no doubt we will hear more of Jessica and her war on drugs. She has a wonderful ability to see beyond the obstacles in life, to focus on the possible and the good. Her life, already, has been a miracle.

A Sandwich for Millie

Karen Olson

Often, as I speak to people who serve others, I find there has been a decisive moment in their lives when they said to themselves, "I won't stand by idly anymore—I'll do something!" Rarely is that moment clearer than in the life of Karen Olson, who began with a simple, spontaneous act of kindness and went on to build a national volunteer program that has touched thousands of lives.

A S A CHILD, Karen Olson believed instinctively that people should care not only about themselves and their families but about everyone around them. Growing up in affluent Darien, Connecticut, the daughter of a successful building contractor, Karen attended the Presbyterian church, but something there didn't feel right. She thought a church should be a place where people reached out to one another, but her church seemed cold and formal, and no one was reaching out as far as she could see.

When she visited her grandmother, who lived near 112th Street and Amsterdam Avenue in New York City, she encountered a world very different from affluent Darien. She saw street people, the kind who would later be called "homeless" but then were usually called "bums" or "winos." One day, when Karen was about twelve, she and her grandmother were out for a walk and Karen noticed an old man in ragged clothing, carrying his belongings bundled in plastic bags. He was shuffling along the sidewalk, stopping every few moments to turn toward the Cathedral of St. John the Divine and mutter a few words, perhaps of prayer. Karen said to her grandmother, "Let's help him." But her grandmother replied, "No, leave him alone—people like that want to be that way."

Recalling that moment, Karen told me, "So my heart began to harden—it was easier to pass people by after that."

Karen's heart never truly hardened, but soon she was busier living her own life than worrying about other people's. She married, had two sons, divorced, and in the early 1980s was living in Summit, New Jersey, and working as a consumer promotions manager for the Warner Lambert Corporation. She loved her job, yet she had a troubling sense that, at the end of the day, all she'd really done was make more money for Warner Lambert.

Though she worked in New Jersey, she often went to New York, where she began to notice the growing number of street people. Sometimes she would see a group of them gathered beside Grand Central Station, and she noticed that the group included an elderly woman.

One day in 1981 she saw that woman sitting on a crate, and although she was late for a luncheon meeting Karen impulsively crossed the street to a deli, bought a ham and cheese sandwich, and gave it to her. The woman touched her hand and said, "God bless you!" and Karen lingered to talk with her. The woman's name was Millie. She was in her seventies, and probably had psychiatric problems, but as she talked about her children Karen couldn't help thinking that if you went back far enough Millie was much like everyone else. She realized, too, that giving Millie a sandwich was probably less important than giving her human contact.

"I reached out to her from my heart, not my head," Karen says. "My head came later. I talked to her and realized that we had a common humanity that was more important than outward appearances. I'd been afraid to talk to a homeless person. So many people are still afraid of them."

Karen went home and told her sons, Brad and Doug, who were twelve and ten, what she had done. "They thought it was great," she recalls. "They said, 'Mom, why

can't we help other people like that?' Children are naturally compassionate. They had the same instinct to help
that I'd had as a child. I thought, 'Yes! We can!' "

On Saturday, Karen and her sons made two dozen
sandwiches and on Sunday they roller-skated around Central Park giving them away. They learned that many homeless people gathered in the Port Authority bus terminal and
they began taking sandwiches there, and getting to know
the people they met. A man named Arthur still had the
medals he'd been awarded during World War II. Abe had
recently had triple bypass heart surgery. Lucille, who once
had been a schoolteacher, and carried a kitten in her bag,
had mental problems. On her good days she would tell
Karen's sons how important their education was. On her
bad days she screamed abuse at them. Soon Karen and her
sons, aided by friends and neighbors, were taking a hundred sandwiches to the bus terminal on Sundays, as well
as clothes they'd collected and information about social
service agencies.

At Thanksgiving, Karen invited some of the homeless
back to her home for dinner, and in the summer she
brought them out for picnics. "I remember thinking,
'Karen, this is nuts—this is *not* the thing to do! You don't
bring homeless people to Summit, New Jersey.' And then I
thought, 'No, this *is* the thing to do!' "

In 1983, Karen attended a meeting of Governor Tom
Kean's Task Force on Homelessness and learned that families were the fastest-growing category of the homeless. She
looked around Summit and surrounding Union County
and found there were two shelters for the homeless and
they were turning away families because they didn't have
room for them all.

Karen attended church only occasionally, but she
found herself wondering if Union County's religious com-

munity knew about the homelessness in their midst. "I thought, 'The churches should want to help these people. It's part of the Judeo-Christian tradition.' " In October 1985, after several months of preparation, Karen convened a meeting of two hundred local religious and lay leaders. She arranged for the founder of the National Coalition for the Homeless to speak. She invited another speaker as well, a homeless woman named Wendy whose husband left her. Wendy had a small child and her newborn baby had died while she was homeless. Listening to Wendy's story, Karen thought, broke down some of the stereotypes of the homeless as mental patients, alcoholics or drug addicts.

Karen and local ministers began meeting regularly to develop a program. They considered a program to renovate rundown housing for the poor, only to encounter the NIMBY factor—people who responded "Not in My Backyard!" when a shelter was proposed too close to home. The clergy realized that their churches contained many rooms that were mostly empty all week, but the churches were not prepared to become full-time homeless shelters.

An idea began to emerge: If they banded together, all the churches and synagogues could do what no one could do alone. Karen recalls, "We were looking for space, and we thought, 'My gosh! Doesn't God want His churches to provide hospitality to people in need?' " The group agreed that churches could take turns giving shelter to the homeless. Soon ten churches and a synagogue had agreed to rotate, each taking a group of homeless people for a week at a time. That meant that each congregation would open its doors to the homeless about every eleventh week.

Although the churches wanted to provide overnight shelter, they could not care for homeless people during the day. The Elizabeth, New Jersey, YMCA agreed to be the daytime shelter. The pieces began to come together. Local social service agencies would screen and refer homeless families to the program. The churches would take three to five homeless families at around five in the evening and provide them with dinner and a place to sleep. Two volunteers would remain overnight at the host site. After the guests had breakfast the next morning, they would pack a bag lunch and return by van to the day center, where they could shower and go on to work or school, or to seek work or visit social service agencies. The emphasis on serving families—no single men or women were included—was decreed in part to focus on homeless children, but also because some potential volunteers were fearful of homeless men, or of the stereotype they had of them.

The ten churches and the synagogue became known as a "network" and Karen's program came to be called the National Interfaith Hospitality Network. A local auto dealer, Autoland, sold the network a van for half price. The Hyde and Watson Foundation contributed $8000 to help with expenses. At the outset, some churches and synagogues had declined to join the network. Perhaps the minister or rabbi was skeptical, or the congregation wasn't sure. But members of those nonparticipating congregations began volunteering in the ones that did participate, and became so excited about the program that they went back to their churches and urged their participation. After a year, by the fall of 1986, enough of the nonparticipating congregations had changed their minds to start a second network in Union County.

"The key is the passion of the people in the pews," Karen says. "There is a hunger in people's hearts to help others. Compassion is alive and well in America. But people are busy—they need vehicles."

Soon religious leaders from nearby Morris and Essex counties asked Karen's help in starting a network. "By then I'd written a handbook for volunteers," Karen says. "I was speaking in churches. I began to see that the program was replicable." As Karen saw it, there were certain fixed elements that every program needed: churches to provide space and volunteers; social service agencies to support the program; a van to move people about; and a day center, which in their first network was a YMCA and elsewhere often was a big downtown church that had declining membership, had plenty of space, and needed a new mission. Karen became convinced that each network needed a paid, full-time director. The programs were simply too detailed and demanding to be run by a volunteer, however dedicated.

Karen began NIHN as a national program in 1988 and it spread rapidly across America. By 1998, more than nine hundred congregations were participating in sixty-three networks in twenty-four states, and others were forming in a dozen other states. Since the program began, more than 85,000 volunteers have helped serve more than 52,000 homeless people, about half of whom are children.

Karen says that about half the people who come to NIHN for housing have jobs but don't earn enough to afford rent. She estimates that the program has helped about seventy percent of the people it serves find permanent housing. She is also proud that NIHN volunteers have gone on to start some sixty related "outgrowth" programs, in such areas as tutoring, health care, restoring housing and counseling.

Her sensitivity toward the people her program serves is reflected in a training film that she narrates for program volunteers. The film shows interviews with people who have participated in the program, both as hosts and as guests. Essentially, the film offers sensitivity training for volunteers. Don't stereotype people, it says, or offer unsought advice, or make quick judgments. Don't talk about "homeless people" or "you people." Respect the guests' privacy. Don't assume that you deserve their life story in exchange for a meal and a bed. Respect their rights as parents. In short, be friendly, be natural and don't be condescending. And don't think you're going to change anyone's life in one evening, because you are not.

NIHN now has an annual budget of nearly half a million dollars a year, all from private donations, corporations and foundations, and she hopes to see that double. Karen is the program's paid director and has a full-time staff of five and a part-time staff of four, supplemented by college interns and volunteers. She says it costs NIHN about $15,000 each time it goes to a city and organizes a new network.

Karen travels around the country speaking to community groups that want to start networks. Before she goes to a city she urges that a local pastor call a meeting of local church leaders. One person, however dedicated, can't start a network, she says. She urges the local people to form a core group to get the program started. Some communities can't overcome local "turf battles," but about two thirds of those she visits do start networks. She tells them that, in addition to the volunteers, they must raise about $50,000 a year to operate a network. That will go to pay a director, as well as rent for an office, insurance for the van and liability insurance for the host churches, telephone bills and the like. She estimates that, thanks to free space in churches, volunteer services and donated food, it costs about $9.50 in administrative costs for each homeless person who stays in a church overnight. This, she says, makes the program one of the most cost-effective ways anyone has found to provide the homeless with food and shelter.

It isn't hard to see why NIHN has succeeded. Ultimately, the reason is that there are so many people in America who want to help others if they're shown a way to serve. But the program's rapid growth is also a testament to Karen's combination of compassion with experience in business and marketing. Her compassion drew her to the problem of homelessness, and her business savvy enabled her to sell her ideas at the national level.

My hometown of Columbus has one of the most active NIHN programs in America. Much of the credit for the success of the Columbus program goes to Richard Stowell, a businessman whose involvement with the homeless in many ways paralleled Karen Olson's.

Richard began volunteering in Columbus homeless shelters in the early 1980s. By the mid-eighties he became aware of the rise in homeless families and wanted to do something to help them. He looked around the country for models and discovered Karen's program in Union County. He had been thinking along the same lines, that churches, particularly suburban churches, were a vastly underutilized resource, in terms of both space and potential volunteers. Unlike Karen, Richard didn't call a community-wide meeting. Instead, in the fall of 1988, he began going to see the pastors one at a time, asking if he could present his idea to their congregations. Most congregations, once they heard his plan, agreed to take part.

"People in churches will respond if they're given a program they're comfortable with," Richard says. "Most people are more comfortable on their own turf, in their own church. The volunteers can reach out in a way that is comfortable, convenient and nonthreatening."

Richard started four networks in 1989 and two more in 1990, and helped other cities in Ohio start their own programs. "The Church of the Master United Methodist in Westerville became our first host church when the network officially began operation in January 1989," he recalls. In the early days, he says, there was a good deal of confusion. Cots traveled from church to church with the families and didn't always arrive on time. "Sometimes the beds didn't get picked up. Then I had to get a U-Haul and draft whatever help I could find to get them moved."

Richard decided to close down his environmental consulting company and devote himself full time to the program. He could afford to do so financially and, as a single person in his fifties, he could make a major commitment of his time. By 1992, after directing the program for four years, he was burned out, ready to move on to something else, so he arranged for the local YWCA to take over the program. He then began working in a program that helped people with drug and alcohol problems. In 1997, to be near his daughter, he moved to San Diego, where he now works for a program that helps women who are domestic violence victims or have substance abuse problems. "Same work, different place," he says.

"Richard had a vision," Karen Olson says. "And he was dedicated. Relentless, really. He said, 'I don't want one network, I want six.' He pounded on church doors, literally. He was the rare exception, an unpaid volunteer who could make a program work."

The YWCA took over the program in October 1992, and now operates as the Columbus Interfaith Hospitality Network. Under this new leadership, the six networks grew to seven, involving 110 congregations, which has doubled the volunteer base. In 1996, the Columbus program served 610 families with more than 1300 children. Its officials are particularly proud that the seventh network, based in downtown Columbus, has given the program more racial diversity.

The YWCA's Faith Mission serves as the Columbus

program's day center. Homeless people gather there, are driven to one of the host churches, then return to the mission the next morning. No one is turned away, because the program has backup shelters to call upon. Although the program does not assume that churches will have showers, some of them have remodeled and added showers, underscoring their long-term commitment. When people return to the Faith Mission, they are offered help in finding housing, as well as classes in parenting and nutrition.

I visited the Faith Mission one night and talked to leaders of the Columbus IHN, including Gwyn Stetler, its director, Sara Neikirk, the YWCA's director of program development, and Rita Cohen, the program's director of education. We visited two churches, the First AME Zion Church and the North Broadway United Methodist Church, where I talked to both volunteers and guests. In both churches, the enthusiasm and dedication of the volunteers was obvious, as they hurried about fixing dinner, entertaining children and organizing sleeping arrangements. It was clear that IHN was an ideal way for individuals with limited time to help those in need, and for churches and synagogues to work together to transform scriptural values into real action.

"We all feel a need to give something but in a busy world we all feel limited," Rita Cohen said to me that night. The beauty of the IHN program is that it enables individuals, and congregations, to take on just what they can handle.

Gwyn Stetler stressed that the experience of working with the homeless causes many volunteers to ask questions about why the problem exists and what can be done to get at its roots. "Volunteering can have a troubling impact," she says. "It starts people thinking."

Karen Olson agrees. She thinks that, as social problems worsen, outstripping government's ability to cope with them, private citizens are stepping forward to fill the gap. Karen is proud of NIHN's volunteers, but as she sees it, providing food and shelter to the homeless is only the start. She thinks the program is educating thousands of people. "Many of our volunteers become advocates," she says. "They look at the problems and begin to see causes. The program changes how they read the newspapers, how they think, how they vote. Public policy advocacy is an important part of what we do."

Karen receives hundreds of letters from those who have taken part in the program, including ministers, program directors, volunteers and guests. Here's what some of them have said.

"I can't begin to put into words what IHN has meant to us. It has become the focal point for renewal in the life of our church. It has generated a whole new spirit of cooperation and generosity among our parishioners. It's given us a whole new vision for what the Church is."
—Rev. David Evans, Shepherd of the Hills Presbyterian Church, Austin, Texas.

"This allows people to do something about their faith. In considering our involvement, we asked, 'What would Jesus do?' In taking part, we have received much more than we've given."
—Dr. Jim Legge, Bullcreek Presbyterian Church, Natrona Heights, Pennsylvania.

"Most of our members live in an isolated, very affluent part of town. The 'poor and homeless' could very easily become just a concept for which we pray each Sunday. IHN brings real people into our lives whom we would otherwise never know. It is a win-win situation. The home-

less receive a home and we receive Christ in receiving them."

— Robert Vickery, St. Michael's Episcopal Church, Austin, Texas.

"The Network program teaches us that the solutions to community problems are in the hearts and minds of the American people, right within our own communities. When we become involved with our next door neighbor, problems become real to us."

— Barbara Lashley, volunteer, Christ the Good Shepherd Church, Houston, Texas.

"I found myself homeless unexpectedly. I'm a college graduate with a major in piano and a minor in voice, two young daughters and a third child on the way. What I like about our hosts in the Network is that they treat me like a person, not like a statistic."

— Tammy J., guest, Cincinnati, Ohio.

These voices represent thousands of people, all over America, who have become part of NIHN. In sixteen years, Karen has gone from giving that first sandwich to Millie to heading a national program that has involved more than 85,000 volunteers in helping families in need.

I asked Karen what had happened to Millie. "I don't know," she admitted. "One day she just wasn't there. I often think of her. In a way, she's as responsible for NIHN as I am. Before that day, I was just passing people by."

A Warrior

for Peace

Geoffrey Canada

Many of the people I describe in this book have shown moral courage, but few have had to exhibit the physical courage, in the face of violence and constant danger, of Geoffrey Canada and his colleagues at the Rheedlen Centers for Children and Families in New York City. They walk the mean streets of Harlem and other neighborhoods, often confronting angry, armed young men, themselves armed only with their courage and determination to make the world a better place.

YOU WOULDN'T THINK, when you first meet Geoff Canada, that he is a student of violence. At forty-five, he is lean, athletic, articulate and rather dapper, given to monogrammed shirts and handsome cuff links. You might take him for a successful, college-educated young executive—which in fact he is. Yet this man knows violence. In 1995 he published a powerful memoir called *Fist, Stick, Knife, Gun: A Personal History of Violence in America*. The title referred to the progression of violence he has known in his life: from the fistfights he survived as a boy in the Bronx to the epidemic of handgun violence he has known while working with the youth of Harlem since 1983.

You can't convince Geoff that people are violent by nature. He remembers his first encounter with violence, when he was four. His father had left his mother with four young sons to raise. One day, he and his two older brothers were playing in a park when a bigger boy stole his five-year-old brother's coat. When the brothers went home and told their mother what had happened, she was furious. The two older brothers were to return to the park and get back John's coat. But the boy was big, they protested, and they'd get beat up. They would get that coat, their mother told them, or she'd give them a beating ten times worse. To the brothers' amazement, the thief surrendered the coat without a fight.

By the time he was eight or nine, Geoff learned to fight. Older boys would goad the younger boys into fist-fights, but they were fair fights—the boys were the same size, no weapons were used, and no one was badly hurt. Geoff learned that if you stood up to a bully he would often back off. He also discovered that, if you carried your hand in your pocket in some neighborhoods, it would be assumed you had a knife and people would leave you alone. He still remembers the first time a man pulled a gun on him and his teenage friends. Fortunately, in 1966, his friends didn't have guns, or someone almost certainly would have been killed.

Because he was small, and an outstanding student, he had all the more reason to learn to protect himself, because good students were picked on by less successful classmates. Geoff won a scholarship to Bowdoin College, in peaceful Brunswick, Maine. Yet while he was there, he did something that underscores just what the pressures of the streets are like: he bought a gun, a .25-caliber automatic with a seven-shot clip. He didn't buy it for use on campus; he was safer there than he'd ever been in his life. But he thought he needed it when he went home to the Bronx, and had to travel through unfamiliar neighborhoods: new gangs were springing up, and he was scared. So when he went home for holidays, and walked the streets, he kept his finger on the trigger of the gun in his pocket.

"When I look back on the power the gun had over my personality I am amazed," he recalls. Fortunately, he came to his senses, and one day, back at college, he walked to the town dump and threw his gun away. Today, he will tell you what a blessing that was, because in the next few years there were times he is sure he would have shot someone if he'd been armed.

In 1975, after receiving a master's degree at Harvard's

School of Education, Canada began teaching at a private school for emotionally disturbed kids in Boston. He could have had his pick of jobs in education or the corporate world, but Geoff felt a calling to work with troubled youth in dangerous communities, like the one he had grown up in, to help other young people who were as frightened, confused and endangered as he had been. Most of the boys he worked with in Boston had been thrown out of the public schools for violent behavior. He learned that he had to face down the troublemakers, or they would take over the school. It helped that he had become a black belt in tae kwon do, a form of Korean martial arts that emphasizes kicking techniques.

In 1983 he returned to New York City to become the director of the Rheedlen Centers for Children and Families, which offers services to troubled young people and families in Harlem. After more than a decade away from New York, Canada discovered how very much life in the streets had changed. The age of the handgun had arrived. He sees the new level of violence in New York as a result of several factors. First, the state's tough anti-drug laws, pushed through by Governor Nelson Rockefeller, had an unintended consequence. Convicted cocaine dealers received long, mandatory prison sentences, so teenagers were drawn to the cocaine trade, because as minors they wouldn't be as harshly punished. Second, the arrival of crack cocaine in the early eighties led to widespread addiction and an ever expanding market for the drug. As a result, teenagers were soon earning huge amounts of money by selling crack, and because of the violent nature of the drug trade almost all of them began carrying handguns.

The Harlem that Geoff returned to was literally an armed camp. He continues to live with that reality every day. If he angers some teenager, neither his intelligence, his good intentions, nor his black belt skills may save him from being blown away. He knows there are hundreds of teenagers walking the streets of Harlem who are better armed and more dangerous than any nineteenth-century Billy the Kid ever imagined. Increasingly, Geoff find himself thinking less like a human-services executive and more like a military strategist.

"These problems can't be solved from a distance," he says. "There is no safe way to deal with the violence our children face. The only way we are going to make a difference is by placing caring, well-trained adults in the middle of what can only be called a free-fire zone in our poorest communities."

In 1990 the city of New York decided to open a number of "Beacon Schools." The idea was to redesign existing schools to become multi-service centers that would be open afternoons and evenings, every day of the year. The Beacon Schools were part of a "Cops and Kids Plan" that would also put more police on the street.

"It was a sound strategy," Geoff says. "This isn't rocket science. You put more police on the street and you give kids more positive options."

Rheedlen was asked to operate one of the first Beacon Schools, and soon Geoff and his colleagues Joe Stewart and Shawn Dove were walking the streets of Harlem looking for a site. They found the school they wanted on 144th Street near Adam Clayton Powell Boulevard. They selected the school precisely because the neighborhood had such serious problems: open drug dealing, abandoned buildings, junkies in doorways, a huge housing project surrounding it, and almost no social services in the area. It was the kind of challenge that Geoff and his colleagues were looking for.

The week before the Countee Cullen Community

Center (named for an African-American poet) opened, Geoff's colleagues Joe and Shawn reported that a boy had been shot dead right outside the school. They talked for a few minutes about the dangers they would be encountering on 144th Street. "This just shows we picked the right place," Joe declared and their project went ahead.

One rainy evening Geoff took me on a tour of the community center, which offers a variety of services, including job training, family counseling, tutoring, discussion groups, karate classes and arts and drama programs. We stopped in the gym to see a karate class. Geoff himself has taught karate for many years to boys in both Boston and New York, because he found that the discipline and self-respect it engenders makes them less violent, not more. When I commented on how dirty the gym was, Geoff explained the problem. New York's custodial union, which is notorious for getting high wages for minimal work, won't keep the school clean, but won't allow Rheedlen to pay others to clean it.

Another problem facing Rheedlen is that it is required to carry out expensive audits for the federal, state and local governments, which together donate about two thirds of the program's $6.5 million annual budget. Geoff doesn't resent the audits. He understands that public funds have to be accounted for. The problem is that the federal audit is supposed to satisfy everyone, but the state and local governments won't accept it, so he pays for endless overlapping audits. He figures they cost the program—and the taxpayers—thirty or forty thousand dollars a year.

Walking through the school, I saw classroom after classroom filled with kids ranging from first-graders to high school seniors. There was a buzz of learning in the air. We stopped and talked to one boy who was studying the geography of the American West, while another learned about Egypt's river Nile. It was six in the evening and Geoff said this voluntary study hall would continue until nine. Not only was studying good for the kids, he noted, but this was the safest place that most of them could be.

Tough discipline is basic to the program. The violence outside cannot be allowed in. No child can prevent the others from learning. Disruptive kids are handled affectionately but firmly.

In one classroom, kids were talking about the controversial rapper Tupac Shakur, who had been gunned down a few months earlier. Like Elvis fans, they were debating whether Tupac might still be alive.

In another room, adults on welfare were learning to use computers. I talked to a middle-aged man who was struggling to use a computer that many of today's six-year-olds have already mastered. Moved by his determination, I asked what the center meant to him. "It's a second chance," he said. "Maybe I can start my life over."

Much of Geoff's battle has been fought not in the classrooms but outside the school. When the program began, a crack house was operating nearby and, when Geoff complained to the police, nothing happened. His response was to organize the neighborhood until the law-abiding people were ready to stand up to the drug dealers, to offer a united front that would drive them away.

We walked outside together, to the corner of 144th Street and Adam Clayton Powell Boulevard; a year earlier, Geoff told me, it would have been too dangerous for me to stand here. But the crack house and the drug dealers are gone now, and much of the gunfire too.

But not all of it. Geoff knows he's in a continuing battle with the forces of violence. His school and its staff and its classrooms and students are a beacon for all that is good in the community, and naturally they are resented by the drug dealers who used to control the block. Not long ago, someone shot through the window of one of the program's storefront offices on 144th Street while the staff was meeting there. Geoff was away, receiving an honorary degree from John Jay College, when his staff called him. They were shaken. Someone could have been killed. They took the shooting not as a random act but as an attempt at intimidation. "We know we've made enemies," Geoff says. "The drug dealers know how we feel about them.

"In the end, we agreed that we can't close up and leave," he continued. "We can't let them run us away. The important thing that happened is that someone shot through our window and we didn't leave. It's a metaphor for everything we do—you have to dig in, stand your ground."

Geoff and his colleagues see themselves in a battle with drug dealers for the souls of many of the youth they serve. And also in a competition with the jails, which will swallow up young people who run afoul of the law. Geoff tells of a minister who asked a drug dealer how he recruited young drug runners. "Any time they need something, I'm there," the dealer said. "If they're hungry I'll buy them a sandwich. If they want to go to a ball game, I'll buy the tickets."

In other words, the dealer plays the role of the Godfather, dispensing favors even as he corrupts lives. Geoff's passion is to offer young people a better choice, a nobler vision of life, than the drug dealers can, despite all their easy money.

One of Rheedlen's most innovative and ambitious programs is called Peacemakers. It came about as a result of talks Geoff had with his colleague Rasuli Lewis, a big, bearded, gentle man who has been his friend since college.

Rasuli had a dream of going to the United Nations as an ambassador for children. One day he said that the children of New York needed to learn the same skills that UN peacekeeping forces use in the world's trouble spots. The result was the Peacemakers program.

That first summer of 1994 they chose fifty young people from Harlem and Brooklyn to train as Peacemakers. They took them to one of the most peaceful places Geoff knows—the campus of Bowdoin College—for a week of training. Each morning began with meditation and continued with classes in conflict mediation and community organizing. When they returned to Harlem, these new Peacemakers led a march of 500 children and adults, chanting, "What do we want? Peace! When do we want it? Now!"

Each summer another group of students goes to Bowdoin to train as Peacemakers. Upon their return, they are assigned to one of Rheedlen's community centers. At a very minimum, Rheedlen's own programs have to be protected from violence, and schoolyard conflicts can be peacefully resolved. The Peacemakers aren't police, but they do escort younger kids to and from school events and, wearing their Harlem Peacemaker T-shirts, they project a presence in the community.

"We're from the community—people know us," says Eric, a handsome young man of twenty-six who is one of this year's Peacemakers. "We change the dynamic wherever we go. We try to teach people a better way to live than by violence."

Geoff points out that there are now about three hundred former Peacemakers, many of whom are still living in Harlem and providing a force for peace on the streets.

Rasuli adds that some people have gotten in the habit of coming out in the morning and standing on their stoops

Geoffrey Canada

and watching children walk to school. "It becomes something the kids can count on," he says. "It becomes a safe
corridor."

The challenge, Geoff says, is to create a "critical
mass" of those who are committed to peace. Every day, in
so many ways, he and his colleagues are trying to tip the
balance from those who embrace violence and death to
those who embrace love and life. Their philosophy is that
most people are good, even in the worst of conditions, and
given a chance they will join the struggle for a better world.
What they need—not just in Harlem but all over the
world—is leadership to help them in the struggle.

Rheedlen is now undertaking its most ambitious project, called the Harlem Children's Zone. The zone reaches
from 116th to 124th streets, and from Fifth to Eighth
avenues. The goal is to saturate the area with services,
working through schools, churches and neighborhood organizations, until the program has made personal contact
with all the 3000 young people who live there.

At forty-five Geoff Canada is an elder statesman in the
battle to save America's children. When I asked him what
our nation's top priorities should be, he had plenty to say.

"Almost all this mess that exists in our cities can be
fixed," he said. "I believe there are concrete answers to all
our problems—crime, drugs, all of them. In the first place,
not a lot of people are willing to spend their time and energy, in exchange for the limited financial rewards, to work
in this field. But if you want to do something, you must
start by assembling a good team. It's no different from
starting a business.

"The big issue is public education. What will America
look like in a few years if we don't solve the problem of
our schools at a time when it becomes harder to make a

living? The public schools are going in the wrong direction—we must fix the public schools.

"The teachers' unions are a problem. They have political clout. No one wants to take them on. But children aren't learning. Their teachers go home at three o'clock and take the summers off. But the problems don't take the summers off. That's why we're here, and we're doing all we can, but it all starts with public education.

"Personally, I've moved a long way on the issue of school vouchers—government payments for students to attend private schools, including parochial schools. I was never in favor of vouchers. I thought they would weaken public education. But after twenty years of dealing with these problems, I think it's time to add competition to the system. We face a crisis and we have to act—vouchers, a longer schoolday, school in the summer, whatever it takes. That includes letting parents purchase a high-quality education, whether it's a private school or a good public school. I believe in the separation of church and state—but not more than I believe in good educations for our kids."

Along with education, Geoff believes in the importance of teaching young people to work.

"When I was a kid, my brothers and I had to because our mother needed our help. We were amazed later when we found out that people would *pay* us to work. Too many of today's kids don't learn to work. They want hundred-dollar sneakers and they want someone to give them to them, or else they steal them. If they learn to work, they'll work their whole lives. Real work can save kids—real work and being held to high standards. You're trained for a job, you're paid for it, and you're fired if you don't perform. That's why we put so much emphasis on helping kids find jobs."

Rheedlen operates ten community centers like Countee Cullen, and Canada says they've had major success. "Eighty-five percent of the kids we work with stay in school, graduate and go on to college. We don't lose many. Not long ago I was at LaGuardia Airport and this young man in greasy dungarees came up to me. 'You don't remember me,' he said. And it was true, I couldn't place him. 'I was the one who was always getting in trouble. But I work here now, on a ground crew.' He was so proud of his job and what he'd done with his life. I thought, 'That's what keeps me at this job, remembering how proud that young man was.' "

Canada remembers other victories as well. A young man who turned from drug dealing to poetry. Girls who have been victims of abuse but now are learning traditional African dances and other kinds of art and drama. Tenants who drove drug dealers from their building with the help of Rheedlen's organizers. When the program counsels troubled families, he says, they can almost always be persuaded to stay together.

Yet Geoff is the first to admit the frustrations of his job. "You can't control some of the things you care about the most. Not long ago we had a five-year-old girl hit by a stray bullet. It was lodged in her brain. I was so depressed. We didn't know if she'd live or die. I dreaded the funeral— that little coffin—but in fact she not only survived but in a month she was walking. We gave a celebration for her. Three hundred people were there, neighbors, doctors and nurses from the hospital. Everyone gave her a standing ovation. We collected money and sent her to Disney World. It was so moving to see her alive and everyone cheering.

"But a few weeks later another little girl was shot and killed in Brooklyn. There was only a small funeral. We have to stop this. It's a huge frustration. You can make such a difference in one child's life but you can't save another one ten miles away. We need a larger movement in this country to save these children.

"People are walking away from the inner cities. We're seeing the suburbanization of America. The jobs are there, it's safer there, and people go there, blacks as well as whites. All for good reasons—people want to protect their families—but we're changing the fabric of America. Right now, the inner cities face several plagues—AIDS, drugs, guns and violence—and even without those plagues it would be hard to keep hope alive in the inner cities. I'd like to think that Rheedlen is a source of hope and inspiration for people. We try to teach young people discipline and performance. We accept only their best efforts but always with love and respect."

Geoff Canada could have done many things with his life. With his brains and drive and education he could have made a lot of money and lived a long way from Harlem. Instead, he works long hours, and literally risks his life each day, to try to help the young people of New York— and of all of America.

Why? What motivates him? "I could make more money some other way," he says. "But I think of my mother. She told me, 'Geoff, you have a talent. You could use it just for yourself, but I'd be hurt if you did.' I think there's a higher purpose to life. I like to think, when I win some small victory, 'My mother and my grandmother would be proud of me today.' "

His book offers another explanation: pain. The pain he sees in so many young people as they try to cope with a world that is stacked against them, trying to destroy them. The pain he himself feels as he looks out upon a nation of poor children. That pain—and the hope that he can lessen it, can help other young people build a better life—is part of what drives him, along with the inspiration his mother provided.

As president and CEO of Rheedlen, Canada has earned a national reputation. He received a $250,000 award from the Heinz Family Foundation, which honors the late Senator John Heinz III of Pennsylvania. He writes op-eds for the *New York Times* and other publications and has written his second book, on how to raise young men. He is much in demand as a speaker around the country.

Geoff sometimes calls himself a cheerleader. He's also a writer, a fund raiser, an organizer, a strategist, a teacher, a lobbyist, a man driven by pain, and an inspiration to others. Most of all, Geoff Canada is a warrior for peace. That is his gift, and we need more like him if we are to win this war.

Welcome to
The Spot

Linda Jakes

You don't enter teaching, nursing, social work or any of the helping professions to get rich. The rewards lie elsewhere. The biggest reward is knowing that you have helped others live better lives. Sometimes, if you are creative and determined, you are able to break new ground in helping those in need. One such person is Linda Jakes, a dynamic social worker who has pioneered new approaches to helping the mentally ill help themselves.

L INDA JAKES is a social worker with Concord Counseling Services in Westerville, Ohio. Officially, she is its aftercare coordinator for the severely mentally disturbed. I learned about Concord when it faced possible closing because of a plan to merge several of the county's mental health facilities. Because I thought it was a good program, I helped persuade county officials to leave it alone. During the discussions I met both Mimi Sommer, Concord's director, and ultimately Linda Jakes, who introduced me to her program of community living for the mentally ill.

Linda's program centers around a large apartment complex in Columbus, not far from where I live. About forty of her clients have apartments there, and one ground-floor apartment serves as their clubhouse. A sign on the clubhouse wall proclaims WELCOME TO THE SPOT! One Sunday afternoon in the summer of 1997, Linda and more than twenty of her clients crowded into the small living room to talk to me. Most were in middle age and are schizophrenics and manic depressives. Most lived normal lives until illness struck. Some can receive relief from drugs; others cannot. They know that their illness is often misunderstood and most are eager to tell their stories.

Susan, a woman in her thirties, told me, "I suffer from multiple personality disorder. I have nineteen personalities. I'm learning to become aware of who they are. I try to integrate them but they don't want me to. I'm divorced and have two children. I can't get a job—they won't give you a chance." Later Linda Jakes told me that Susan, like most women with multiple personalities, was the victim of severe sexual abuse as a child.

Brian has schizophrenia: "I take many pills every day to control my racing thoughts. I hallucinate. I've been employed—I sweep floors and work part time at McDonald's. I got a perfect attendance award. I live here. The group supports me and I support the group. I feel at home here."

Laura and John, a married couple, sat close together on the sofa. "I had no disability until I was forty," she said. "I worked for a vet and raised quarter horses and Belgian sheepdogs. But now I suffer from depression. It runs in my family. Concord has been life-saving for me. I plan to go back to school. When I function, I'm a high-functioning person. I survive on four hours of sleep a night." John added: "I suffer from obsessive compulsive disorder. If I get into a fight, I'll sulk for twenty-four hours and go over the details over and over. It's part of my personality. Here at Concord, I met my wife. I brought her back from the depths. Now we're functioning."

Joan, a schizophrenic, has been in the program for seven years. She and her friend Cindy organize a Wednesday night film series at The Spot that features movies about mental illness, such as *The Snake Pit, The Awakening* and *One Flew Over the Cuckoo's Nest.*

Jim is a tall, dark-haired, handsome man in his fifties. I had come to admire him during a previous visit to The Spot. He is legally blind, suffers from multiple sclerosis and is a paranoid schizophrenic. Jim has heard voices and seen hallucinations every day of his life. Sometimes the voices are loud and the hallucinations overwhelming. Medication gives him only partial relief. He has had shock treatments three times over the past twenty-five years. I once asked Jim how he had the strength to—as he puts it—"reach for the light every day." He replied in a soft voice, "I read the Bible, and I understand Job."

Everyone praised the work Linda Jakes has done to forge them into a community of friends who encourage and support one another. "This group is my family," some said; others declared, "This group saved my life." The program, which serves a total of about three hundred mentally ill people, is a monument to Linda's vision, dedication and determination. It could be a model for a nation that is still struggling to find effective ways to help the mentally ill, who too often are locked out by society because of fear and ignorance.

That Sunday at The Spot I also met the Randalls, as I will call them, and later they told me their story in detail. Until the summer of 1993 they had been the model of a healthy, happy, successful American family. John and Betty Randall met in graduate school, married and settled in the Columbus area, where John worked as a systems analyst and Betty pursued a teaching career and raised five bright, healthy, college-bound children. If there was any cloud on their horizon, it was that Betty sometimes suffered from periods of depression. But the problem could be treated by medication and she never missed a day of work because of it.

Trouble struck the summer their fourth child, Adelle, was fifteen, and about to enter her sophomore year in high school. Over the Fourth of July weekend the usually reserved Adelle talked nonstop and started making extravagant plans about how she would spend the paycheck she had just received from her summer job. It was disturbing behavior, quite unlike Adelle, and her parents called their family doctor. He referred them to a psychiatrist, who talked to Adelle and told the Randalls that she had suffered a hypomanic episode. They could give her medication, he said, or just wait and see what happened. They decided to wait, and Adelle seemed to return to normal.

Nine months later Adelle went to a convention for Latin students. A friend of hers was running for president of the group; Adelle, busy passing out buttons and putting up posters, didn't sleep for two days. When she came home she was laughing and talking loudly. She came to her mother's bedroom at six-thirty one morning to borrow her telephone to call her sister in England. She told her mother that the people in the cars driving by outside had come to see if she'd cleaned up her room.

Adelle's parents took her back to the psychiatrist, who said she was manic depressive, needed medication, and should be hospitalized. Manic-depressive (or bipolar) disorder is caused by chemical imbalances in the brain that cause its victims' moods to swing from depression to extreme elation, or mania, that can bring on hyperactivity, disjointed ideas and recklessness. It strikes a lot of people, as it did Adelle, in their late teens, when chemical changes are taking place in their bodies. Most people who suffer from bipolar disorder respond well to the mineral salt lithium, which somehow evens out the illness's terrible lows and highs, but there is no real "cure" for a chemical imbalance. In the vast majority of cases, it's there for life, and people have to learn to live with it.

Despite the doctor's recommendation, Adelle's parents weren't prepared for the trauma of seeing their daughter hospitalized. They thought they could care for her as well, or even better, at home. She took her medication—lithium—and was fine for the next two weeks, until her parents went to an out-of-town wedding. A couple the Randalls trusted stayed with Adelle. The parents stressed the importance of Adelle taking her medicine, but when they returned three days later she was catatonic and barely knew who she was or who her parents were. She ran away, and the police had to find her and bring her home.

Again, the psychiatrist recommended that Adelle be hospitalized, and again her parents could not bring themselves to take that painful step. Instead, they turned their home into a hospital. They put locks on the doors. Adelle's father slept on the floor outside her bedroom at night to make sure she didn't escape. They were afraid that if she got away again she might run into traffic or otherwise do harm to herself. Some nights she stayed up all night dancing, while one of her parents watched.

"Manics don't sleep," Betty says. "In the nineteenth century, sometimes they would die of exhaustion."

Still, Adelle completed her sophomore and junior years of high school successfully, except for periodic depression about her classwork.

In the summer before her senior year Adelle attended a journalism conference out of town. The sponsors assured her parents she would get plenty of sleep because the students had to be back in their dorms by eleven each night. Unfortunately, once back in their dorms, they stayed up all night. By the time she came home, Adelle was acting strangely again.

Nonetheless, the Randalls set out for a family reunion in Maine. "The trip was a disaster," her mother recalls. Adelle became extremely competitive with her cousins. She was upset if she didn't win when everyone played charades at night. She began waking up early, always a bad sign. Fearing another manic episode, the family started home. "It was the drive home from hell," her mother recalls. Adelle talked so loudly in one restaurant that they had to leave. When her brother played a tape she didn't like, she began hitting him. In the motel, their first night on the road, she stayed up all night, and the second night she ran to the lobby in her pajamas.

By the time they reached home her parents had finally decided she must be hospitalized. Adelle sobbed hysterically when she realized what was happening. Yet hospitalization worked. Given a sedative, she slept for twenty-four hours, getting the rest she needed, and after a week she was able to return home and start her senior year in high school.

Adelle had been appointed coeditor of the school paper, but she had a disagreement with the other editor and the school authorities dropped her. She lost interest in school—it was a battle to get her to go each day. Still, she graduated, and because of her good grades and high test scores she had scholarship offers to two colleges.

She decided to go to Ohio State University. She didn't want to live at home, however, and her parents didn't want her living in a dorm. "A dorm is a manic environment to begin with," her mother says. One of her brothers offered to solve the problem by sharing an off-campus apartment with her, but this well-intentioned plan backfired. Adelle began cutting classes and falling behind in her work. In February she told her parents she'd gotten a job and met some girls she wanted to move in with. Her parents, glad to see her making friends, did not recognize another manic episode coming on. Before she could make the move, Adelle disappeared for twenty-four hours. Her parents finally found her in a bar. They called the police but they would not intervene unless a person was in a state of extreme distress, and Adelle seemed rational when they arrived. Her father and brother stayed with her in an all-night Kinko's copying center.

The next morning they took her forcibly to a psychiatric hospital and persuaded her to enroll there for three weeks, but she hated it and was no better when she left. Two weeks later she moved in with the girls she'd met, who had no idea of her problems. After two nights, one of the girls called Adelle's parents. "You've got to come get her—we don't know what's wrong with her." Her parents found her in a coffee shop. "She had a haunted look," her mother recalls.

Her parents told her she had to go back to the hospital. Out on the street, Adelle began to fight them and scream. A passerby warned that he was going to call the police. "Fine, call them," her mother said. "We need help."

They finally got Adelle to the psychiatric hospital, where it took six attendants and a sedative to get her under control. Then a nurse told her parents, "You must never do that again—you kidnapped your daughter." Adelle was nineteen and in the eyes of the law an adult—her parents had no right to force her to go to the hospital.

After three weeks of treatment Adelle moved back home, in April 1997, and began to do better. She slept well, finished one of her English courses and worked as a volunteer for a theatrical company. She dated that summer, spent time with friends, got one job and lost it, got another job, and made plans to return to college in the fall, while continuing to live at home.

Both Adelle and her parents remain hopeful. "I think I can deal with it," Adelle says. "I need to see my doctor and take my medicine and adjust the medicine. I can tell when I'm getting manic. I get giddy—that hectic flush—and excited. I hope someday I can live without medication, because we don't know all the possible long-term side effects. There are periods when I feel completely okay. I might have future episodes but I hope they can be taken care of quickly and I can return to normal life." Adelle isn't ready to make long-term plans, but when she eventually graduates from college she thinks she might like to teach English at the high school level.

Adelle's illness has been agonizing for her and the Randalls, as it would for any family. Her parents want to give her as much freedom as possible, yet they never know when she may become a danger to herself. Still, the Randalls have been lucky in one regard. John Randall has excellent medical insurance, through the company he works for, and it has covered virtually all his daughter's medical expenses, including psychiatrists, medicine and periods of hospitalization that cost as much as $5000 a week.

Already, they are deeply concerned about what will happen when Adelle turns twenty-three and is no longer covered by her father's insurance. Adelle worries about whether she'll be able to find a job that will provide the coverage she needs. With all her other troubles, it's not something she should have to worry about.

Adelle and the others I've described are the kind of people Linda Jakes is trying to help with her program of group treatment for the mentally ill. She understands that mental illnesses tends to isolate people. Many people are afraid of the mentally ill, or unsure how to deal with them—they avoid the mentally ill far more than they would those with physical illnesses. For their part, the mentally ill are also afraid, and ashamed, and too often hide from the world. This isolation only makes their condition worse. Linda's inspiration was to bring them together, as tenants in the apartment complex, and as friends in The Spot, who can support and encourage one another. They help each other cope with their challenges, from taking their medication to hearing voices, for no one understands those difficulties better than they themselves. Their families gain a measure of peace from knowing that their loved ones are not walking the streets or sleeping in cars.

Linda Jakes is a small woman with big talents. She is the kind of person you would turn to in a crisis, someone who can keep her sense of perspective during the most turbulent times. She uses her gifts to the maximum in helping others.

Raised near Toledo, Ohio, Linda attended Bowling Green University, where her early interests were art and philosophy. She entered social work by accident when she happened to pass a university crisis center that was looking for volunteers. She volunteered and, because she liked the social workers she met there, and the work they did, changed her major.

After getting her B.S. in social work, Linda took a job with a private clinic in Norwalk, Ohio, that treated people with severe mental disabilities. Until then, Linda's only personal experience with mental illness had been from time she spent with a wealthy uncle, who suffered from bipolar disorder. Although a successful businessman, he behaved erratically and sometimes had to enter private hospitals for treatment. "I found him fascinating," Linda says. "He would go on buying sprees, then fall into terrible depressions."

But her uncle's experience wasn't typical. His wealth protected him. Most people with mental illness face a far more uncertain future. When Linda began her career, in the late 1970s, she was entering a field that was still very much in flux. For many years America's mentally ill were confined in large mental hospitals that often were overcrowded and offered minimal treatment. In the 1960s a movement began to take the mentally ill out of hospitals and return them to the community, a process that was called "deinstitutionalization." This trend began for at least three reasons: growing revulsion at crowded, inhumane conditions; the high cost of maintaining the mental hospitals; and the development of psychotropic medicines that made it possible for many mentally ill people to control their symptoms and lead more normal lives.

The big problem with deinstitutionalizing, Linda says, is that it was unplanned. "They let people out and gave them a card with a phone number to call—and a lot of them were back in the hospitals fast. There were no resources out there."

When Linda started at the Linn Center in Norwalk as an aftercare coordinator, she found that in this rural area many of the mentally ill lived at home, where they had family support but had no friends or social life outside the home.

"If you don't have social contact, if you're isolated, you're probably going to get worse," Linda says. "You may create a crisis just so you'll have some social contact. So why not give them social contact? Let's go to the zoo. Let's go see a movie. Let's do something as a group. We tried it in Norwalk and it worked. The use of emergency services went down among the people involved in groups. When that happens, you get administrators' attention, because emergency services are expensive. They say, 'Let's expand this.' "

That's what happened in Norwalk: Linda expanded the group program, the clients benefited, and expensive crises became less frequent. It all seems so obvious. I asked Linda why more communities aren't stressing group treatment for the mentally ill.

"If you read the literature," she told me, "it says that most peer group programs don't work. Why? I think because people didn't give them enough time. It may take six months or a year before a lot of clients are comfortable with a group. They've had bad interaction. People see them talking to themselves and walk away from them. They're afraid. The emergency services have become their support system. They need time and encouragement before they can accept a new system made up of people like themselves. It's a proactive approach and we're a reactive society."

After seven years in Norwalk, Linda entered Ohio State University to earn her master's degree in social work. The course took two years, during which she supported herself as a waitress. "Being a waitress is a lot like being a social worker," she jokes. "You're helping people with problems."

In 1987, after receiving her master's degree, Linda went to work at Concord Counseling Services. At the outset, she told its director, Mimi Sommer, that she wanted to expand group care programs, and she has had Mimi's support ever since. At first, Concord was helping about thirty people with mental disabilities; today that number is closer to three hundred. As word of the program spread, more and more people have wanted to be part of it.

When Linda arrived at Concord, four or five of the clients were living at the apartment complex. The manager of the complex had a brother with mental illness and was open to accepting others as tenants. "They tend to be reliable," Linda says. "Some are compulsively neat and they help keep the grounds clean. And if they have a problem, the management knows they can call me or one of the others in the group instead of having to call the police."

Today Linda has nine support groups in operation, each with twenty to thirty members. All use The Spot as their clubhouse. About forty clients live in the complex, with others in nearby apartment houses. Most receive Social Security payments. In addition, Medicare pays for the services that Linda and her staff of seven provide, and most of the clients also receive a housing subsidy from the Columbus Metropolitan Housing Authority that pays most of their rent. Linda's program is officially called the Community Living Project, or CLP, which has inspired the clients to sometimes call themselves the Clippers.

Linda says of herself and her staff, "We go to them. When we get folks hooked into one another, they need less help from us. We hook them up with social resources. We make sure they pay their bills. We help them find jobs. We teach them personal hygiene. We teach them peer support and try to make them functional."

Finding work for the clients is difficult. Some local employers have been good about giving the mentally ill a chance, at least at part-time work, but many still are wary of employees who may at any moment be unable to come to work or may behave oddly on the job. She estimates that eighty percent of her clients are capable of working at least a few hours a week, but only a small percentage of them have jobs, and too many of those are "fast food jobs or janitors."

Linda dreams of creating a job program for her clients. She believes that channeling their energies into work would give them a tremendous boost. To enable them to operate a coffee shop is part of her dream. She knows they hunger to be productive.

For some, the bottom line to Linda's program is that it saves money. Mental patients who encourage one another to take their medicine and solve their crises among themselves cost the taxpayers less money than those who turn up in jails and emergency rooms or back in mental hospitals. To Linda, of course, money is not the main issue. "I think what we're doing is best for the clients and is morally right," she says.

I asked Linda if she had a favorite success story. She responded cautiously, because she knows that mental illness is a lifetime condition, but then she told me about a man who came to her for help in 1987. He was about thirty and had his master's degree in theology, in preparation for reentering the ministry. Then mental illness struck and left him with schizo-affective disorder. For months his condition, and the collapse of all his dreams, left him depressed and suicidal. He spent time in a mental hospital where the doctors warned him he would never be able to hold more than a menial job. They laughed when he said he wanted to be a writer.

As part of his rehabilitation, he moved to the complex and began attending groups four times a week. He stayed on his medication and began to improve. Linda encouraged him to pursue his dream of writing. He went back to school and earned a master's degree in journalism. Today he is a reporter for an Ohio newspaper, hasn't been in a hospital in five years, and plans to write a book on mental illness. Linda, who still sees him once a month, beams with pleasure as she recounts his story.

I asked Linda if she is ever discouraged. Not often, said Linda, who loves her work and doesn't have time for negativity. Then she laughed and said there was one time when she was temporarily discouraged.

"I had a client who was having a crisis and I was trying to get her to go to the hospital with me. Finally she said, 'I'll come if you'll buy me a grape pop.' I got her into the car and went to a store and bought a grape pop—and she poured it on my stereo. When we get to the hospital they won't take her—they say she's not homicidal or suicidal. Meanwhile, she goes into the bathroom and locks herself in. I try to persuade her to open the door and finally she does. But by then she has urinated in a cup and she throws it in my face. At that point the doctor says, 'Okay, we'll take her!' So I'm driving home, and I smell bad, and my stereo won't play, and I was pretty discouraged—for about an hour. But I got over it. She was one of my favorite clients."

Linda is far too busy and dedicated to stay down for long. She doesn't know of another program in the country that is doing as much to encourage community living and peer support among mental patients. "We don't just give them entertainment," she says. "We create a more normal existence through peer support. If they have a problem, we teach them not to call emergency services but to call a peer."

Having seen Linda's program in operation, I can testify to its compassion, and to the fact that it works. I hope other communities study what Linda is doing. Mental illness is no different from the physical illnesses and disabilities that we have grown to understand. It can strike any American family, but too often we run from it and treat the mentally ill as outcasts. Linda is one of those who is showing us a better way.

In 1996, Senator Pete Domenici wanted to pass legislation requiring health insurers to offer mental health parity—to equalize coverage for mental health services with coverage for physical health services. In other words, a person who becomes manic depressive would have equal coverage with someone who developed cancer. Most health insurance plans don't offer the same level of coverage for mental and physical health services, and they oppose parity because they say it would increase the costs of premiums.

Pete Domenici was chairman of the Senate Budget Committee, as I was chairman of the House Budget Committee. He feels strongly about parity because a member of his family suffers from mental illness. When he asked for my support, I said I would lead the fight in the House.

I told House Speaker Newt Gingrich that I intended to push the mental health legislation. He respected my wishes, although we both knew that it wouldn't be an easy sell. The health-care industry was in strong opposition and many of our Republican colleagues were skeptical. I would have preferred for the industry to come forward with a voluntary plan for parity, but they did not, so I felt Congress should act.

Our efforts were successful. The Mental Health Parity Act because law on January 1, 1998, and requires annual and aggregate lifetime dollar limits to be the same for mental health coverage as for physical health coverage. The law isn't perfect. There are more limits on the coverage than we wanted. But it is a start, and will make life easier for the people Linda Jakes helps at The Spot, and others like them all over America.

I Want to Save the World

Ana Rodriguez

I never tire of visiting Philadelphia. It's a city of elegance, humanity and history. Colonial architecture pervades the historic district: you half expect to see Ben Franklin hurry out of City Hall and hop into his carriage. Church steeples point like narrow fingers to the sky. The mix of poverty, history, tough blue-collar neighborhoods and wealthy suburbs gives Philadelphia a special intensity. It was there that I met Ana Rodriguez, whose courage in facing her past has given thousands of other women hope for the future.

ANA RODRIGUEZ is a tall, attractive, articulate and highly regarded police officer in Philadelphia. Today she exudes self-confidence, but that was not always true. Two decades ago Ana lived with a man who beat her severely. For years she lived in fear, unable to understand why no one would help her, almost convinced that she was herself to blame. Now, thanks to her remarkable strength of character, she has not only turned her own life around but dedicates herself to saving other women from the abuse that she knows all too well.

Ana's parents moved from Puerto Rico to Philadelphia before she was born. At sixteen she began living with a Hispanic man. "At sixteen you think you know it all," she says now. "Within a year I was pregnant. That was when the beatings began. My son was born when I was seventeen. After that the attacks became worse. He would beat me, bite me, kick me, give me black eyes, rape me, lock me in a room. Once he hung me out a second-floor window and threatened to drop me. He always said it was my fault, that it was because of things I did, and I accepted his excuses. At first I would fight back, but that only made it worse. I learned to take the beatings and keep quiet.

"When I called the police, they would see my black eye, my split lip, but they would say, 'He's your husband, you have to listen to him, learn to get along with him.' Once I told the policeman, 'I was asleep and he woke me up and started beating me—how was I to blame?'

"I was always afraid. Petrified. When my parents found out, they thought the beatings were my fault too. I left him many times but I would always go back. He threatened my parents and in part I went back to protect them. I also went back because I thought I could heal him. Women are raised to heal. I thought I could change him.

"But there was no pleasing him. He was Latin, he was macho. He was raised that way. His father beat his mother. It's about power and control. It's a man's way of saying, 'I'm the king—you must obey me!' Sometimes he would cry after he beat me. One he gave me some matches and said, 'Burn my hands—I've got to stop this.' He felt great anger, and he had a problem with drugs and alcohol.

"The police, the neighbors, my family, everyone said I was at fault. Sometimes I thought they were right. Once I saw a psychiatrist and she said I must be paranoid, must be exaggerating. She wanted me to take Valium. Sometimes I felt like I was going crazy. What is most painful now is realizing what my son went through. To live with that hurts a child emotionally. The end came when he beat our son. He was beating me, and our son, who was about three, came forward to protect me and he hit him. I hit the man with something and knocked him down. When I went to see if he was okay, he sucker-punched me. I woke up in the bathtub, wet and bleeding.

"I got my son and caught a bus to New York. I remember how people looked at me—I had blood all over me. In New York, I stood in the bus station for four hours, not knowing what to do. I didn't have any money. Finally I called my parents and they said I should come back home and stay with them. At home, it was like I was a prisoner in my parents' house for a year. I was afraid to go out by myself. I was afraid of what he might do to me or to my family. Finally he found another victim, another woman, and I thought I might be safe from him. I'd been with him for five years. I think if I'd stayed much longer he would have killed me."

Ana went back to high school and got her degree. She took some college courses and became the manager of a department store. Her father encouraged her to take the test to join the police department, which she did in 1987. She graduated from the Police Academy and was assigned to patrol duties. "At first, I didn't tell people about my past. Then one day I responded to a domestic violence call. It was a young woman with a child, like I had been. She said, 'What do you know about it? You're a cop!' So I told her my story."

In 1990 she joined the victims' assistance program, which helped all victims of crimes, including domestic violence, and in 1993 she moved to the department's newly formed Domestic Violence Unit, which focused exclusively on family members—not just spouses or lovers—who abused one another. By then, things had begun to change. Police were less likely to ignore women who said their husbands beat them. New laws had been passed and were starting to be enforced. An officer didn't have to witness the domestic violence in order to make an arrest. Ana's job was to follow up every report of violence against a woman and offer her help. She urged abused women to consider their options, which include leaving the man and bringing charges against him.

"You really can't understand it unless you've been through it," she says. "Why do they stay? Out of fear. Because it's cultural. For financial reasons. Because of the kids. Out of shame. Or because they think they love him. Domestic violence is a cycle. The woman loses self-esteem. He makes promises and she wants to believe them. Statistically, women leave five to seven times before they leave for good. I left five times. I realized I had to talk about my past to make it heal."

Over the years, investigating hundreds of cases of abuse, Ana has seen it all. "I've lost two women in five years, killed, and I take it personally. The two men, one killed himself, the other is in prison. Another woman, the ex-husband slashed her throat; she survived and he's incarcerated now. Some women have had a finger cut off. Some are beaten unconscious. I deal with a lot of emotional trauma—I keep up contact with the women.

"They want the abuse to stop but not the abuser to leave, for whatever reason, economic or because they think they love him or can heal him. So they go back. They want to believe he'll stop. But we'll see them again if he's not held accountable. The men go into the honeymoon stage—'I love you, I'll stop it'—but then it starts again.

"More women are prosecuting, bringing charges. We let them know they're not by themselves, that they don't have to live this way. But whenever there's a domestic violence homicide we lose a lot of them. The headlines scare them. They say, 'She had a protective order and it didn't save her. I better go back to him—I don't want to wind up dead.' So many still believe it's their fault. The husband tells them it's their fault. Some cultures tell women they should be subservient to men. We're slowly changing that. Men need treatment as well as punishment. It's easier to change the law than to change attitudes."

Ana says there are two times in particular when women are at risk of abuse. The first is when they are pregnant. "The man doesn't know what will happen. She's not the same person. He's insecure. He thinks she may not love him anymore. He feels financial insecurity. Anger. And she is more vulnerable. She can't fight back. That's what happened to me. I had to protect my unborn child."

The other dangerous time is known to most Americans as Super Sunday. "This year, I did a radio show on the day of the Super Bowl, warning women about abuse. It's the combination of men drinking and gambling and getting angry when they lose their bets. They take it out on the women."

I asked Ana if many men were getting counseling and if it helped.

"Men get treatment but no accountability," she told me. "The judge sends them to an 'anger management' class but the quality of treatment isn't good and they don't change. They just get a piece of paper signed.

"We need to reach the kids. I started a program called Positive Rap. I go to schools and we do role playing. I ask them what a relationship should be. 'Is it okay to hit your girlfriend?' So many boys say yes. They say, 'I have to keep her in line.' He thinks he's the king of his castle. That's what they learn at home. Unless we change that, we're raising the next generation of abusers—and victims. Sometimes I ask the boys, 'Would it be okay for some guy to beat your sister?' They're not so sure about that. We try to talk to them about love, about what a relationship can be. When we raise kids, we have to teach them to be human beings first."

Ana introduced me to Flo, who works as an administrative clerk in a Philadelphia hospital. Over lunch, Flo told me about her daughter Diane, who at age thirty became involved with a construction worker who had emotional problems and who abused alcohol and drugs. When Diane tried to break off the relationship, the man terrorized her and her mother. This went on for five years. He would call in the middle of the night and threaten to kill them. He would slash the tires on Diane's car. If she went out with another man he would harass and threaten him.

He would send Diane women's underwear that had been slashed to pieces. He wrote Diane's employer and urged him to fire her, claiming she was a thief and a drug abuser.

Flo often called the police, but time after time they said there was nothing they could do because they hadn't seen the crime committed. Even after Flo got a court order, the police did not stop the man from terrorizing the two women. "We lived in hell for five years," Flo says.

"When I met her, I found her story hard to believe," Ana says. "I was angry. Everything she said was true. She had the letters she'd written to judges and the police but nobody had arrested him."

"I told her, 'Don't bother, they won't do anything,' " Flo injected.

"I said, 'Give me a chance,' " Ana replied. "I got her statement and her daughter's statement, got a warrant and arrested him. The evidence was overwhelming. I talked to the guy when he was in jail. I warned him that if he got out on bail and bothered them it would be a felony for intimidating a witness. I urged him to get counseling."

The man served several months in jail and has not bothered Flo or her daughter again.

"Ana literally saved our lives," Flo says. "No one would do anything and then she had him locked up within a week."

As Flo's case suggests, one of Ana's challenges is to persuade some of her fellow police officers to take domestic violence seriously—because the old ways of thinking are not entirely gone. "I try to deal with them one on one," she says. "I ask them, 'What if it was your sister or mother?' "

In 1997, Ana joined the Philadelphia District Attorney's Family Violence and Sexual Assault Unit, which prosecutes cases of child abuse, domestic violence and adult sexual assault. She is a Detective One, investigating cases of abuse and preparing them for court. She likes this assignment because she thinks that, along with education and prevention, some men need jail to stop their violence against women. Often, she says, men are given six months probation for a first offense, but after that they often serve the time.

Ana's boss, Assistant District Attorney Charles Ehrlich, says of her, "Ana does a great job. She relates very well with victims of domestic violence and she can ferret out the truth about what really happened to make sure we have the facts before we go to court. She combines street smarts with a special sensitivity to people." In recent years, Ehrlich says, the number of domestic violence cases his office has prosecuted has more than doubled. The biggest challenge is getting women to testify against their husbands or boyfriends, and that is where Ana has been so effective.

Ana's job includes some community education work, and beyond that she volunteers much of her off-duty time to her crusade against violence. "I do a lot on my own time. It's important for us to be proactive." She speaks at schools, churches, housing projects, hospitals and community groups. She urges doctors to screen patients for signs of domestic violence. She tells of speaking at a medical school and having a student come up afterward and confess that she was a victim of violence.

"Not long ago I spoke at the Men's Fellowship at a Baptist church, my first meeting with an all-male group," Ana told me. "It was exciting because they were really interested and asked good questions and asked how they could help. The minister said he wanted to do more. There may have been abusers in the group, but no one argued or tried to defend it. It was great—we talked for two and a half hours."

Ana doesn't have much confidence in statistics, but the district attorney's office estimates that there are 40,000 abused women in the city and she has to reason to doubt it. She says that she herself has worked with more than a thousand abused women in her eleven years on the police force. "It's a mistake to think it's only the poor and uneducated," she warns. "It's everywhere in our society."

When she tells audiences about her own experiences, she says, "sometimes I get emotional." She has hundreds of letters from abused women and from people who have heard her speak that testify to the impact she is having. Yet her own father told her he disapproved of her talking about her years as a victim. "I told him it was part of my healing," she says.

Healing has not been easy for Ana. One marriage failed. When we met, she was engaged to a Philadelphia detective but she was postponing marriage until she's sure everything is right. She is concerned about her son, too, and the scars he bears from his early years.

Ana is a tough professional, yet she has a vulnerable side, even a girlishness; her joy for life shines through the grim memories of her past and the hard realities of her work today. It is inspiring to see a woman who has lived through such a nightmare emerge so strong and optimistic, with such a wonderful sense of caring. Ana is one of those heroes who not only can survive adversity but can grow strong in the face of adversity. She knows the enemy and is determined to defeat it. As she made clear, this isn't her work, it's her life. For the future, she talks of returning to college and getting a degree in psychiatry or social work to better understand the causes of abuse and how to deal with it.

I asked Ana if she is ever discouraged by the endless panorama of violence she sees. "Yes, sometimes it's overwhelming," she said. "I see so much suffering and I think, 'How far have we come?' I have bad days. But then I get a call or a letter from some woman I've helped and I can see hope. I want to save the world, but I realize I have to save it one woman at a time. Sometimes I get emotional when I tell the people about the pain I suffered. It's hard. But the only way we heal is to go back and understand what happened. Sometimes I get tired of telling my story, but then a woman says, 'Thank you, you've helped me,' and it's all worthwhile. I believe God put me here for a reason and the reason is to help people deal with this problem."

Demanding
Excellence

Gertrude Williams and
Charles Beady

Trudy Williams is the principal of the Barclay School, in Baltimore, and Charles Beady is president of the Piney Woods Country Life School, near Jackson, Mississippi. Although they have never met, they are partners in a crusade for a better education. What unites Charles and Trudy is a fierce belief that, if underprivileged students are challenged, they will meet the challenge. Charles and Trudy have the courage to demand excellence and the passion to inspire it.

G ERTRUDE "TRUDY" WILLIAMS is a five-foot ball of fire. I loved her from the moment I met her. Trudy's title at Baltimore's Barclay School is principal, but teaching is her life and the entire community is her classroom. She is a warrior for righteousness, who will risk everything for her beliefs, and that has enabled her to change thousands of lives.

Trudy grew up in Philadelphia, where her father was a contractor—a good builder, she says, but a poor businessman. Her mother took in laundry to help make ends meet. "We were poor but not destitute," she recalls. "We went to school and went to church. My mother would say, 'If you really believe in something, just ask God for direction and no one can tell you how far you can go.'"

After graduating from Chaney State College, a Quaker school in Pennsylvania, Trudy began teaching in Baltimore's then segregated schools. In the 1970s she was made assistant principal of the Barclay School, which serves grades K–8 in a neighborhood of aging row houses, closed-down factories and street-corner drug sales. Most of its students are African-American children from disadvantaged families whose low incomes qualify them for the free lunch program.

When Trudy arrived at Barclay she found student test scores well below the national average and teachers who had become demoralized by teaching "fads" that came and went every few months. Teachers, too, came and went. In short, the school was in chaos. It was on life support. "I thought, 'We've got to find something new. This isn't working. There isn't any structure.' Everyone was doing his own thing. There were no stated goals. There was no understanding of what a kid has to do to learn. Someone would tell them to write a story, but they didn't know how to write."

Trudy reached out to the neighborhood, going from door to door to enlist parents in their children's education. "If you have a weak family, a strong school can help pull them together," she says. Slowly, things began to improve. After she had become Barclay's principal, in the 1980s, Trudy saw an opportunity for dramatic change when she served on a committee that Mayor William Donald Schaefer set up to improve Baltimore's schools.

"A friend on the committee suggested that I go look at the Calvert School," she recalls. "I went there and it was so exciting to see kids reading and working and studying. It was heaven. I came back and told the steering committee, and others went to the Calvert School and they were just as excited."

The "heaven" that Trudy discovered was a private school, located about three miles away, that for almost a century had been teaching the children of Baltimore's most affluent families. The Calvert School was proudly old-fashioned. It ignored fads and stuck to the basics. Students practiced penmanship, wrote essays every day and were expected to learn math and read literary classics. Teachers were there to teach and students were there to learn. Discipline was enforced. Test scores were high.

It was Trudy's dream to apply the Calvert School's demanding curriculum to her students at the Barclay School. As it happened, officials of the Calvert School and

Baltimore's Abell Foundation had also been wondering if Calvert's rigorous methods could be used effectively in public schools. After Trudy joined the discussions, the Foundation agreed to donate $100,000 a year for four years to implement the Calvert curriculum at Barclay. Among other things, the money would pay for a Calvert teacher to work full time on the program, special training for all teachers in the program, and textbooks and other teaching aids.

To Trudy's dismay, Baltimore's superintendent of schools opposed the Calvert-Barclay plan. He argued that the private school curriculum wasn't appropriate for Barclay's students and that the money should be divided up among many schools, rather than lavished on one. But Trudy possessed a crucial weapon. After a decade of reaching out to parents, she had the neighborhood behind her. She could mobilize community support. She could turn out a crowd of loyal, vocal supporters at a school board meeting. The battle went on for eighteen months. In one famous exchange, the superintendent declared that a "rich man's curriculum" was not suitable for Barclay's students. Trudy angrily replied, "I'm not about to give them a poor man's curriculum—we've already got that!"

Trudy fought so vigorously and outspokenly that her friends feared she would be fired. "They would say, 'Let us fight this one.' But I was six feet tall. I was determined, because our children deserved more. You can't say they can't learn. You have to give them the same playing ground. You have to have the same expectations that you would if the child was a Rockefeller."

The debate was decided when Baltimore's new mayor, Kurt Schmoke, sided with Trudy. "You deserve a chance to try," he told her.

The Calvert-Barclay program was initiated in Septem-

ber 1990, when the new curriculum was first given to kindergarten students. Each year, another grade was added.
By 1997 the first class of students to enter the program had
reached the eighth grade, and the seven grades behind were
following along. (When the first grant expired, the Abell
Foundation made another, also of $400,000, to continue
the program for another four years.)

The curriculum stresses reading and writing. Students
write an essay every day and rewrite it until the teacher
deems it perfect. Classes are no larger than twenty-five students, and teachers' aides help focus individual attention
on each student. Volunteers assist with tutoring and reading programs. The volunteers include students from Johns
Hopkins University and parents from the Calvert School.
Trudy particularly stresses the involvement of students'
parents.

"I have never met a parent who didn't care about their
child, but they have different ways of showing it. I meet
parents who have been so beaten down that they can't
help. But it's our responsibility to teach them. Some
houses, you go to and wince. But you sit down and talk.
You work with them. And I let them know that I'll take
them to court if their child doesn't come to school."

Students are regularly tested and their scores com-
pared with those in the classes just ahead of them—
including their own brothers and sisters—who aren't in the
program. The results have been dramatic. Those not in the
program tested mostly in the twentieth to the thirtieth percentile in reading, writing and math. Those in the program
score at, or above, the national average, often rising as
high as the sixtieth percentile. In other words, those confronted with a demanding curriculum met the challenge
and improved their scores twenty to thirty points above
those not in the program.

Those are the numbers. To tour the Barclay School with Trudy is to see the human side of the equation. All the clichés about poor kids in urban schools are quickly exploded. The students wear dark pants and skirts, and white shirts, and march from class to class in single file. Wall posters proclaim things like HUGS, NOT DRUGS. Inside the classrooms, when the teacher asks a question, students eagerly wave their hands, pleading to be called upon. Neatly written essays are posted on the walls, with a photograph of each author. Trudy points to the erratic handwriting in one essay. "That could be a sign of trauma," she whispers. "We'll keep an eye on it."

In one class the students were divided into two teams answering questions about *Robinson Crusoe*. When the teacher asked "How long did Crusoe stay on the island?" each team huddled, fiercely debating its answer. "Twenty-eight years, two months, nineteen days," one team's captain declared—the right answer, the teacher confirmed. It was inspiring to watch the children competing, proud of their knowledge, waving their hands for recognition.

School attendance is up since the Calvert-Barclay program began, and teachers report few discipline problems. Those problems arise, Trudy says, when kids are bored. If you engage, respect and challenge students, they repay you with good behavior and hard work. "The work ethic has changed," she says. "Teachers say, 'I don't have to pull teeth now—I get something back.' The kids *want* to learn. They're like sponges. They don't want to go home. They come around in the summer, when school is out, and ask what they can do."

The students themselves praise the program. Most view it as a springboard to a better life. One girl, asked if her friends razzed her for studying so hard, replied defiantly, "They can say anything they want—they'll be the ones working at a supermarket and I'll be the one with a good job living in a big house."

In the fall of 1998 the program faces a new test, when the Barclay eighth graders, after nine years of preparation, enter Baltimore's public high schools or, in some cases, attend private high schools on·scholarships. Trudy believes the solid foundation they received at Barclay will enable them to continue to excel in high school and will help propel them to college.

Trudy herself will have retired by then, after forty-eight years in the Baltimore public school system. For all her achievements, she is still angry about the faults of the public school system. "The biggest problem in education is that the money goes everywhere except where it is needed. The saddest part is that you can't get the money into the classrooms." As she sees it, she's been fighting for more than a decade to protect her program from the "downtown" administrators who want to scuttle it. "The school has to fight its own administrators to preserve its excellence." She vows that the battle will go on. "I won't be gone. I'll fight them from the outside now!"

The Piney Woods Country Life School, located on a 2000-acre campus twenty-one miles from Jackson, Mississippi, differs in many ways from the Barclay School in Baltimore. It is a private school, serving three hundred students in the seventh to twelfth grades. Both schools believe that discipline is basic to academic excellence, but Barclay begins working with children of five or six, when they are more easily molded, while Piney Woods takes in teenagers, whose habits and attitudes may be more difficult to change. On the other hand, Piney Woods students live on campus twenty-four hours a day, away from home and hometown distractions. But, at heart, the two schools face their different challenges with the same philosophy: if you demand excellence, you will receive it.

The Piney Woods School was begun in 1909 by a remarkable man named Laurence Jones who, after working his way through the University of Iowa, caught a train for Mississippi, carrying with him a few dollars, a Bible, two books on farming—and a dream. Here is how he explained it later:

"I decided to share my advantages with the neediest people of my race in the Black Belt of Mississippi. There was the most shocking waste of all: the waste of the human mind and soul. Men, women and children exhausted their bodies in the fields, making their living as farmers but having no knowledge of farming beyond the drudgery of chopping and picking cotton."

Amazingly, Laurence Jones raised the money, reached out to both black and white communities and built his school, a day and a dollar at a time. Eventually the school's focus changed from educating black students from the Jackson area to attracting "at risk" students from all over America.

In 1954, Jones's tireless fund raising was supplemented in a most unexpected way. When he was featured on the popular television show, "This Is Your Life," host Ralph Edwards asked viewers to send a dollar to support the Piney Woods School. More than $750,000 poured in, which became the school's endowment. Jones wrote and thanked everyone who had contributed, and many sent additional donations.

Today, Piney Woods has an annual budget of more than $7 million. It obtains money from its endowment and from a combination of individuals, churches and foundations, all of whom believe in the continuing importance of this school. Traditionally, white Mississippians have been instrumental in the school's financial survival, but in recent years its funding has become more national in scope and more racially diverse.

The school's endowment, which was $18.5 million in 1985, has climbed to $31.5 million today, in part because of good investments and the bull market of recent years. Few students pay the school's full tuition of $8300 a year; most pay about $2000, with the school making up the difference. Fund raising is a constant challenge.

Much of the recent revitalization of Piney Woods has flowed from its third president, the vigorous and charismatic Charles Beady. Beady grew up in Flint, Michigan, where his father worked in a Chevrolet plant. "My father would beat the devil out of me," he says. "I was scared to death of him. I studied hard and stayed out of trouble. He would say, 'Don't bring home any C's—they're as close to the bottom as the top!' "

After being elected president of his senior class in high school, Beady entered Michigan State University, where he received his B.A., an M.A. in urban counseling and a Ph.D. in education. He studied under Professor Wilbur Brookover, the father of the effective schools movement, who taught that all kids can learn and that the entire social and psychological climate of a school determines how well they learn. The key to successful schools, he said, is to have principals who demand excellence of teachers, who in turn demand excellence of their students. Beady had begun an outstanding academic career, with posts at Johns Hopkins University and Morgan State University, when in 1985, much to his surprise, he was approached about becoming president of Piney Woods. Fate had taken this young scholar from the knee of Wilbur Brookover to a school in rural Mississippi where he could test the master's theories on a grand scale.

"I came down here on a lark," Beady says, "but I fell in love with Piney Woods. This is a holy place."

Beady came to Piney Woods at a time when historically black boarding schools were facing hard times. Once there were nearly a hundred of them in America, but with the coming of school integration they began to die out. Today, Piney Woods is the largest of just six that remain.

Beady took a hard look at Piney Woods and saw that much work was needed. Physically, it was a school where the trash was still picked up by a mule-drawn wagon. Socially, a new generation of teenagers was challenging the school's traditions. Beady decided that firm discipline was essential to transforming at-risk youngsters into the college-bound scholars who were his goal. "My first year, we suspended eight students. If they won't work or study or follow the rules, they have to leave. It can be heart-wrenching, but my philosophy is the greatest good for the greatest number. If you start bending the rules, everything falls apart. We drag them kicking and screaming toward excellence."

Beady took Piney Woods back to the future. Students are expected to dress neatly and study hard. Boys cannot wear the earrings and baggy pants that may be fashionable back in the 'hood. Most classes last two hours and there are mandatory study halls at night. Students work ten hours a week in school offices, food services, groundskeeping, or on the school's 500-acre working farm. They must take part in daily chapel services. Fighting, drinking and even public displays of affection are not permitted. A girl who became pregnant was suspended just before graduation. Some students protested when the school decided to place surveillance cameras around the campus, but the cameras stayed.

Beady believes in motivating students by word and

deed. A visitor to the campus sees signs which feature the school slogan:

Fame Is Vapor
Popularity an Accident
Riches Take Wing
Only One Thing Endures: Character!

Beady's deep feelings about proper behavior were seen a few years ago when he felt that some senior girls had worn dresses that were too revealing to their prom or had danced with their dates in unbecoming ways. At the next Sunday's church services he was overcome by emotion, tears glistening in his eyes, as he reminded the seniors of their obligation to set a positive example for the younger students.

Most Piney Woods students come from poor families and are considered at risk of academic failure or delinquency. Their backgrounds include broken homes, parents who abuse drugs, and communities where gang violence and drive-by shootings are commonplace. Piney Woods takes these kids and with a combination of tough love, encouragement, faith and teamwork transforms them into the best they can be. Students often say that at first they resented the school's boot-camp atmosphere, but in time they understood it was good for them.

But Piney Woods isn't all discipline and hard knocks. The school's sports teams have distinguished themselves, as have its Cotton Blossom Singers, who have delighted audiences all across the state. Since Charles Beady arrived at Piney Woods, two new girls' dorms have been built, one of them thanks to a donation from cartoonist Charles Schulz. It is known affectionately as Snoopy Hall. Another donor was Oprah Winfrey, who gave money to hire a social worker.

The size of the student body has doubled, to about three hundred, since Beady arrived, and the school has opened a full-time day care center which serves its more than 150 employees and the surrounding community. A Junior ROTC program was begun in 1992, has won many honors and has seen its leaders go on to full scholarships at leading colleges.

Not surprisingly, Piney Woods (like the Barclay School) stresses writing skills, with a program called Writing Across the Curriculum. Students keep daily journals and carry out writing exercises in all their classes. Tutoring programs serve those who need extra help, and a college-level computer science lab has been established as well.

The school demands excellence and the students meet the challenge: virtually all Piney Woods graduates go on to college. Some are admitted to high-prestige universities and colleges such as Princeton, Harvard, Smith, Oberlin and the University of Chicago, while others attend outstanding historically black colleges such as Tuskegee, Morehouse and Grambling. Moreover, Piney Woods officials say that, of their graduates who enter college, about two thirds earn their bachelor's degrees, and one third of those graduates pursue graduate degrees. That is a remarkable record for a school whose mandate requires that sixty percent of its students come from low-income families.

When I visited the school with my friend Mike Parker, who represents the district in Congress, Beady arranged for us to talk to a group of students. Here is part of what they had to say:

Kenyatah Masterson, of Washington, D.C., told us about the difficulties caused by her mother's drug use. For her, Piney Woods has offered stability.

Rasheedah Noble, from San Jose, California, said she'd stayed in a homeless shelter with her father for several months before coming to Piney Woods, and although she had to work hard the discipline was good for her.

Jermaine Blackwell, of Mayorsville, Mississippi, told us, "If I was at home, I wouldn't be studying and looking into my own soul. I'd be hanging with a gang, doing bad things, maybe selling crack."

Ben Berryhill, Piney Woods' only white student, said he'd been suspended from high school back in Fort Smith, Arkansas, for fighting, once chased his brother around the kitchen with a butcher knife, and probably would have dropped out of school and run away from home if he hadn't entered Piney Woods. "When I got here, guys looked at me like I was crazy," Ben recalls. "It was an interesting time. But now it's fun."

These are some of the kids Piney Woods takes. Not bad kids, but kids who need discipline and special care. And they get it. Piney Woods was a miracle when it was founded in 1909 and it remains a miracle today. It takes teenagers who would likely drop out of high school and transforms them into college-bound young men and women. It salvages young lives because Charles Beady and his associates have the courage to demand discipline, hard work and excellence—and because they believe that "at risk" youngsters can rise to meet the challenge. Piney Woods is an old-fashioned school built on old-fashioned truths: that hard work and discipline are the "secrets" of success.

Going far beyond the call of duty, Trudy Williams and Charles Beady don't just educate young people, they raise them. They give something of themselves to each child, and they are energized by the effort. By molding the present, they help to shape the future. Words alone can't thank them, but when others are inspired to follow their example, they receive their greatest reward.

Their successes put to shame the pessimists who say that millions of young people must be written off because they come from broken families and tough neighborhoods. Despite the obstacles, the young people have the innate capacity and desire to learn. The question is whether our schools, educators and communities have the wisdom and courage and dedication to make them learn.

Angels' Place

Loretta Nagle

*When I met Loretta Nagle, she reminded me of
Donna Reed, the star of the 1960s hit TV show
that bore her name. Loretta, like Donna, looks
like the perfect wife, mother and neighbor. Yet
she's also a strong woman who, while raising a
large family, began a career as a nurse, then
started an ambitious program to help the developmentally disabled. The program is called
Angels' Place, and Loretta is the angel who
made it happen.*

L ORETTA NAGLE was the youngest of seven children. Her mother died when she was two and she was raised by her father, a doctor in Detroit. As a girl, Loretta wanted to be a nurse, but her father disapproved—and his word was law. For a time she thought about becoming a nun but instead, at eighteen, after one year of college, she married Terry Nagle, her high school sweetheart, and they proceeded to have seven children in ten years. Terry supported the fast-growing family on his income as a salesman of automobile parts. "Don't ask me about the Vietnam War," Loretta says, "because I missed it."

When Loretta was thirty-four and her youngest child entered school, she returned to the dream she'd surrendered nearly twenty years earlier: she entered nursing school. She received her degree at forty and started working part time as a nurse. By then, Terry had switched from selling auto parts to manufacturing them and was becoming highly successful.

Through her forties and early fifties, Loretta worked part time as a pediatric nurse, volunteered at an inner-city clinic, enjoyed an active social life with old friends from the University of Detroit, and watched her children grow up, marry and have children of their own. It was a good life, but by the early 1990s Loretta was restless. Nursing was no longer a challenge. "One night I was in bed and I was really sad and I said, 'Lord, you'd better use me, because I no longer have any children to care for and nursing just isn't doing it for me.' Within two weeks I met Annemarie in the hospital cafeteria."

Annemarie Lopez and her husband had three children, two boys and a girl. Although the boys were healthy, her first child, Charlotte, was, in medical terms, "profoundly disabled." Annemarie never knew precisely why. She had a difficult labor and they gave her drugs that she thinks might have harmed her baby. Or it's possible the doctor may have misused the forceps. For whatever reason, Charlotte was born with bruises on her head, and the first thing her mother noticed was that her baby didn't cry. Charlotte didn't learn to walk until she was four. She grew into a woman whose intellectual level is about that of a normal three-year-old. She is social, she can express joy and sorrow, but she uses only a handful of words—"mama," "car," and a few others.

Annemarie and her husband cared for Charlotte at home but it wasn't easy. Sometimes Charlotte cried all night and the only way Annemarie could quiet her was to take her for long drives. After missing a night's sleep, she would go to her nursing job at the hospital. As she neared sixty and Charlotte entered her thirties, Annemarie worried about how long she would be able to care for her daughter. Then she happened to talk to Loretta Nagle in the hospital cafeteria.

They were both Catholics, both in their fifties, both nurses at the William Beaumont Hospital in Royal Oak, outside Detroit—yet they didn't really know each other. Loretta knew that Annemarie had a developmentally disabled daughter and she asked how she was doing. As they talked over coffee, Annemarie explained that her greatest fear was what would happen to her daughter if she, the mother, died or was disabled, or simply became too old to care for her. Hundreds of other parents of adult developmentally disabled children shared the same fear, she added. There was virtually nowhere for the children to go except to foster homes. Some foster homes were all right, she said, but others were operated by people who were only in it for the money. Even if the foster home was a good one, it was a terrible shock to a developmentally disabled person to be suddenly put in a new environment. Sometimes the stress of such a move led to death.

As the two women talked, Annemarie told her, "It's too bad we don't care for our own the way the Jewish people do." Loretta asked her what she meant, and Annemarie told her about the Jewish Association for Residential Care, which operated twenty homes and apartments for the developmentally disabled in the Detroit area. The disabled included those with Down syndrome, others who were autistic, and those with brain damage and other disabilities at birth that left them with an IQ of less than seventy.

When Annemarie mentioned the Jewish Association program, Loretta thought of her friends Rosemary and Dan Kelly, whose son had been diagnosed with a mental illness. Dan was a successful business executive and they had spent huge amounts of money to place their son in a program in Connecticut. Recently, they had raised money to start a home for him and others with mental illness on a farm called Rose Hill, there in Michigan. That night Loretta called Rosemary and asked how she and Dan had raised the money to start the home for their son. Rosemary pointed out that a program for the developmentally disabled would be different from a program for the mentally ill, but she said the money was out there and she would help Loretta and Annemarie any way she could. Loretta couldn't quite believe what was happening—she didn't even know Annemarie's last name—but she wanted to help her and the next day she sought her out and told her what her friend Rosemary had said. Soon the three women met in Loretta's kitchen and Rosemary talked about organizing and fund raising. "She said, 'You two can start a program,'" Loretta recalls. "We didn't know what she was talking about."

The project took on a life of its own. Loretta and Rosemary had contacts in Detroit's business, political and religious worlds, and Annemarie had a passionate desire to provide a home for her daughter and others like her. They met regularly and Annemarie began writing a proposal to submit to Adam Cardinal Maida, the Archbishop of Detroit. Loretta, Rosemary and Annemarie met with the cardinal, joined by two other mothers of adult children with developmental disabilities, Peggy Prentice and Margaret Maxwell. The cardinal encouraged them and suggested other sources of funds, but after a year they had made little progress and they returned to him and asked if the Church would donate ten wooded acres it owned. At that time their dream was to build ten homes for the developmentally disabled on the ten acres. The cardinal agreed to donate the land—and then the women discovered their plan had a serious flaw. In addition to whatever private funds they could raise, they needed government money to operate the program, and mental health officials didn't like their ten-acre plan. The trend in care for the developmentally disabled, as for the mentally ill, was to move them out of large institutions and into the community. Their plan to build ten homes on ten acres, and keep the disabled isolated there, was to public health officials a step in the wrong direction.

Meanwhile, they had gone ahead with plans to kick off their project—now called Angels' Place—with a meeting at the Birmingham Country Club. Cardinal Maida, their featured speaker, was to announce the gift of the ten acres. At the last moment their planning group decided they couldn't accept the ten acres and would have to return to their earlier plan to buy ten homes in ten parishes in the Detroit suburbs. Loretta met the cardinal at the door of the country club and broke the news. She was amazed at how calmly he stood before the audience of three hundred a few minutes later and announced the new plan. As I said to Loretta, when she told me the story, cardinals tend to be quick on their feet.

"The thing you have to understand," Loretta says, "is that we were ignorant. We knew nothing. We made major mistakes but the Lord corrected them. We would be wondering, 'What next?' and things would happen. We had a golf outing and raised $44,000. Someone gave us an anonymous $50,000 pledge. A man I'd never met donated his office, which was worth $80,000. A woman who'd read about us called and said she had a perfect home for us that she'd sell us at a bargain.

"About that time, a priest, Father Murphy, called and said he knew a woman who was dying of cancer and needed a home for her son Frank, who was thirty-two and had Down syndrome. We met with the woman. Her husband had deserted and left her with five boys. She said, 'As soon as I was diagnosed with cancer, a year and a half ago, I started praying for a place for Frank to live.' I think that woman prayed Angels' Place into existence. Frank became the first resident of our first house, Saddlewood. Two months later his mother passed away."

Loretta became the program's director of development. "I'd never asked anyone for money in my life," she says. But she believed in her cause and she wasn't shy. She had read that columnist George Will had a developmentally disabled son, so she called him and he agreed to speak at Angels' Place's first fund raising dinner. His appearance drew a crowd of 850 people at $150 each, and the event netted the program about $70,000.

Major contributions came from many Detroit corporations and foundations. The Kresge Foundation made a $150,000 challenge grant, based on Angels' Place raising an additional $1.65 million. In all, the program has raised more than $3.5 million dollars in five years: about twenty percent from foundations, forty percent from individual donations and forty percent from corporations and special events. Loretta proved, as others have before her, that Americans have big hearts and amazing generosity when they see a real opportunity to help.

By the start of 1998 the program had six homes in operation: two they had bought, one they built, two that were donated, and one that is owned by a resident's father. One of the newest Angels' Place homes serves inner-city residents in a historic residence in downtown Detroit that Cardinal Maida donated. The homes are attractive, well-furnished residences that anyone would be proud to live in. Each holds from two to six residents, has a home manager and two or more care givers, at least one of whom is there around the clock. The six homes are now occupied by a total of thirty residents. Loretta estimates that it costs as much as $40,000 a year for each resident, so there is constant pressure to raise more money. Most residents can contribute only their $600 a month Social Security payments; in addition, they receive Medicare and Medicaid benefits. As Loretta sees it, Angels' Place is in a partnership with the county and the federal government, which contribute about two thirds of the cost of the program. Her goal is for Angels' Place to contribute the houses and about $125,000 a year toward their operation, while the county and federal governments contribute staffing and transportation.

The program deals with strong passions and often with desperate people. Loretta tells of mothers driven to leave their developmentally disabled children on doorsteps, or even to kill the child and themselves when they had no way to care for them. It is agonizing for Angels' Place officials to have to choose the few people they can give a home to from among the hundreds in need. Much of this work is done by the program's three paid administrators: Executive Director Cathleen Gilbert, Director of Program Services Cheryl Loveday and Administrative Assistant Deborah Chappa.

When I visited Angels' Place, I met both Frank and Martin, the first two residents of the first Angels' Place home, Saddlewood. Martin is a man in his sixties who was abandoned at birth. He had lived in orphanages and foster homes all his life. For more than ten years he had been with a couple who fed him poorly and left him alone much of the time. His sister read about Angels' Place and called to ask if they could help. Board member Pat Hurlbert, a nurse, investigated and urged that Angels' Place take Martin in.

"We were just getting started," Loretta recalls. "We wanted Martin out of there and with us. But we didn't have any money to provide for him. Then Pat Hurlbert suggested that we call the Knights of Columbus and see if they'd fund him for a year. The man there said, 'It's funny you called. It's the end of the year and we have some extra money. How much do you need?' I asked for $17,500 and it came the next day. It was a miracle."

Meeting Martin and Frank gave me a glimpse into the world of mental retardation. Their disabilities make it impossible for them to compete in a fast-paced society that too often lacks compassion and sensitivity. But they have the gifts of childlike honesty and unique powers of observation. That is why we can learn from them and why we have an obligation to, as Loretta says, "end the neglect and prevent them from being shoved to the background."

For all the developmentally disabled, entering a new home is difficult, and every effort is made to involve the parents in the transition. Annemarie Lopez's daughter Charlotte now lives at Webster Home, in Southfield, with four other profoundly disabled women. Her mother is tremendously proud and pleased. "Charlotte's life has special value," she says. "She inspired this whole program." Still, it was not possible for Charlotte to be one of the program's first residents. The first two homes took in less severely disabled residents. The program needed more experience before it could deal with profoundly disabled people like Charlotte, many of whom communicate very little and some of whom are in wheelchairs. The program had to build a house specially designed for them, with extra-wide hallways and doors.

Even then, Annemarie says, the transition was hard. For the first eight months after moving in Charlotte barely left her room. But now she is doing well. Most days she goes to a job where she performs simple tasks. The care givers take her and her housemates on walks and to the zoo and shopping malls. Each woman has her own room: clean, bright, festive spaces, decorated with dolls, stuffed animals, bright paintings and pictures of family and friends. You cannot but be moved when you see the level of love, comfort and companionship these women, and all Angels' Place residents, receive.

Pine Center, in Bloomfield, has been open since the spring of 1996 and is home to two women: Mary Beth, who is thirty-three, and Michelle, who is thirty-seven. Michelle's father, Alan Miller, a lawyer and former professional football player, owns the house. The home manager is Sister Pat (Patricia Kolbiaz), who greets visitors with a hearty: "Welcome to our palace—these are the princesses!"

The two women, less severely disabled, are indeed princesses in this beautiful house. They eagerly show their rooms and tell about their work and social lives. During the day Michelle keeps Pine Center tidy and Mary Beth works in a church kitchen. Evenings and weekends they and Sister Pat are busy with movies, softball, shopping trips, bingo, bowling, aerobics, dances and social events with others in the program. One of the goals of Angels' Place is for the residents, as much as possible, to share the pleasures that others in society enjoy, and to a remarkable degree that goal is being achieved.

Whenever Angels' Place has gone into a neighborhood they have encountered initial resistance. "First you buy the house, so it's done," Loretta says. Although the law is on their side, they gladly meet with the neighbors to ease their concerns. Sometimes the neighbors say they don't mind women residents but they fear that men will be a menace. Sometimes they are worried about property values. In the end, they always conclude that Angels' Place is a good neighbor. The home managers make a point to plant flowers and keep the yards neat. When there are neighborhood cleanup programs, the residents are enthusiastic volunteers. Open houses are held and questions answered. In the end, there are no problems.

For the future, the board hopes that Angels' Place can expand to ten homes. They met with a group of parents in Grand Rapids who have started a program modeled on Angels' Place, and Pat Hurlbert produced a video the program uses for fund raising and to send to interested groups in other cities. One of the biggest concerns is the future of the program. The initial board of directors was mostly made up of friends of Loretta and Terry Nagle, all about the same age, but now they are bringing younger people onto the board. Angels' Friends, a group of younger supporters of the program, now has more than 300 members. Loretta says that the vast majority of their supporters have had no personal experience with developmental disabilities, but when they become aware of the problem they want to help.

In the future, Loretta believes, Angels' Place must become an advocate on behalf of all developmentally disabled people. In addition to the relatively few to whom it can offer a home, it should lobby for more funds and services for those who are still living at home or in foster homes. The disabled and their families are often unsophisticated people who do not know how to negotiate with agencies and often get no help at all. For those in Angels' Place, as for those in many other programs, volunteerism leads to advocacy.

Loretta's personal goal is to withdraw from fund raising and devote herself to the spiritual development program. "I think our residents should have lives like other people have and access to all the things that everyone in America has access to. They should participate in the community to the best of their abilities. They should live in nice homes like we do and work and earn money if they can. Most importantly, I think they should have an opportunity to have a personal relationship with the Lord, just as we can.

"We have monthly spiritual development meetings. They're small, private and voluntary. We talk about the Lord. We share prayer. One time Frank was angry at Mark and he prayed that he wouldn't be. We sing. Frank has a beautiful voice. We have a talented volunteer, Monica Mylod, who plays the piano. When our residents pray, you see the Lord in their faces. We can't begin to give these guys as much as they give us. You start out to do this good thing, but it's overwhelming what you receive back. There's so much joy. They've given me a closeness with the Lord that I never knew I could experience. I've never been happier. I have endless energy. I feel blessed that this has come to me."

How many people have been blessed because two nurses, Loretta and Annemarie, met for coffee one day. The most wonderful part of the story is that Loretta is no different from you or me. She is a mom, a wife and a nurse. What she has accomplished is amazing, but it's not beyond the reach of any of us if we give ourselves a chance.

The Cookie Lady

Cheryl Krueger

There are many kinds of courage. Courage can mean standing up in the face of evil, or it can simply mean the courage to dream your own dream, to go your own way. You may not think Cheryl Krueger belongs in this book. She doesn't operate a homeless shelter or work with AIDs patients. Cheryl makes cookies. Starting with a dream nearly twenty years ago, she has built a multimillion-dollar gourmet food company. In the process she has become a special kind of business executive, one who thinks not only of profits but of what she owes to her employees, her customers and her community. Let me tell you about her, and maybe you'll agree that she, too, is both a model and a hero.

C HERYL KRUEGER grew up on a farm in northern Ohio. Her father was a farmer and her mother worked in a manufacturing plant for many years. The greatest influence on Cheryl in her girlhood was her grandmother, Elsie Krueger, who lived with the family after the death of her husband, Cheryl's grandfather. Elsie met the school bus every day when Cheryl came home from school, and then the two of them would often settle in the kitchen, where Elsie taught her granddaughter to cook and bake. In Cheryl's mind, baking cookies in that kitchen with her beloved grandmother became a kind of Eden that later in life she would seek to recreate. Elsie was a businesswoman as well. Each day she drove a truck to a nearby town to sell butter and eggs door to door. With her profits she bought the fabric that she used to make the family's clothing. This remarkable woman lived to be ninety-eight and was able to see her granddaughter, inspired by her example, achieve far greater business success.

When Cheryl graduated from high school her parents thought she should stay on the farm, marry some nice young man from the area and live the same life they had. Cheryl had other ideas, and managed to attend Bowling Green State College by holding down two part-time jobs. At first Cheryl was a home economics major, thinking she would teach, but her part-time job in the clothing store took her to New York one summer and provided her with

a glimpse of a bigger, more challenging world. After graduation she took a job with a Miami department store. But
wanting to live closer to home, she returned to Ohio in
1976 to take a job with The Limited, a huge chain of clothing stores with headquarters in Columbus.

In some ways it was a very good job. She was well
paid, and she traveled all over the world selecting mer-
chandise for The Limited's stores. "The problem was I had
no control over my life," Cheryl recalls. "I had no social
life. I was in my twenties and I didn't have a date in four
years." That was an astonishing situation, since Cheryl is
as beautiful as she is intelligent and self-confident. But she
was a prisoner of her success. In 1980 she took another,
even higher-paying job as vice-president for the Chaus
clothing company in New York. But soon she wanted out.
She had seen too many divorces, too many colleagues who
never saw their children, too much office politics and back-
stabbing.

Besides, Cheryl had a dream.

She wanted to make cookies.

At heart, she wanted to recapture the warmth, the
sense of belonging, the sense of control of her own life that
she had known when she was a child baking cookies with
her grandmother. "When you grow up on a farm, you feel
that you're in control of your own destiny," Cheryl says.
"That translated into me wanting to have my own business—essentially it's the same thing."

She had noticed gourmet cookies springing up around
the country—Mrs. Fields, David's, Famous Amos—and
she thought she could make better cookies than any of
them. She talked to David, of David's Cookies, who said
he would sell her a franchise for Columbus for $250,000.

Cheryl was shocked. "What do I get for all that
money?" she demanded.

"The use of my name," David explained.

"But nobody in Columbus has ever heard of you," Cheryl replied.

Cheryl decided to follow her dream on her own. For several years, while her cookie company was in the planning stage, she continued to work in New York and commuted to Columbus on weekends. She put $40,000 of her savings into the venture. Her first employee was a close friend, Caryl Walker, whom she'd first known in college. She gave Caryl five percent of the company and trusted her to run things when she was away. Next, she hired her brother Jim, whom she entrusted with actually making the cookies.

They were set to open the business on September 1, 1981, when disaster struck. Test runs of small batches of their cookies had been delicious, but when they made their first large batch the cookies were awful. Cheryl didn't know what the problem was, only that her cookies were inedible. Their customers were waiting, their money was running out, and they had no cookies.

Desperate, Cheryl rushed into a Columbus restaurant and asked to speak to the chef. "I need your help," she told him. "I don't know what's wrong with my cookies!"

The chef promised to come to her office the next morning. ("I'm so lucky to live in the Midwest," Cheryl says. "He was helping a total stranger.") It took the chef only a few minutes to spot the problem. Cheryl and Caryl had been measuring the ingredients with the kind of scales you use in a grocery store for weighing fruits and vegetables. It was fine for that, but not precise enough to translate a small batch of cookies into a huge batch. The chef told her to go buy digital scales. Cheryl did—charging the $500 to her credit card—and once again her cookies came out delicious.

Cheryl's Cookies grew steadily, but in 1985 her friend and partner, Caryl Walker—a vegetarian, a runner, in perfect health—was diagnosed with terminal cancer. It was then that Cheryl quit her clothing-company job to devote herself full time to her cookie business. "We were like sisters," Cheryl recalls. "She died in my home in May 1986. She was thirty-three. I saw her carried out in a body bag. And I thought, 'What's the point of life? We're only here for a short time and you have to leave something behind you. This company is going to do as much good for as many people as it can.' "

Since then, Cheryl's Cookies has continued to grow. In 1986 the company had sales of $2 million. By 1997 sales had reached $26 million and she has set a goal of $100 million by the year 2002. In the process, her three-person company has become a three-hundred-person company that includes a retail business, a mail order business and a wholesale business to airlines and restaurants. But more important than the size of the company is its spirit.

"It may sound sexist," Cheryl says, "but there's a mother running this company and it makes a difference."

Of Cheryl's three hundred employees—"associates," she calls them—eighty-five percent are women. Many are women who would not have been hired or promoted at other companies because they lack formal education. But Cheryl gave them a chance. Hers is probably one of the most family-friendly companies in America. "Whenever possible, we work around a child's schedule," Cheryl says. "If your child has a soccer game or a school play, go to it—just let us know. I remember how important it was to me that my grandmother was there when I came home from school. I want my associates' children to have that too."

She tries to promote from within and to encourage

new ideas from her employees rather than from outside consultants. She formed a President's Club of the company's thirty-five most outstanding employees and last year took the entire group to a three-day retreat at a resort in Jackson Hole, Wyoming. The club doesn't just include top executives: some members are truck drivers and bakers, and at the retreat each was given stock in the company. If Cheryl's Cookies goes public in a few years, as planned, that stock could become extremely valuable.

To tour Cheryl's plant with her is to see what a family operation it is. The receptionist has multiple sclerosis—and her job is guaranteed as long as she can work. Cheryl proudly tells me that her assistant's daughter has just been admitted to Harvard. She points out an employee who is mentally handicapped, mothers who work part time, and a baker who wept when she gave him stock in the company.

Perhaps one reason for Cheryl's success is that she has never forgotten her origins in her family kitchen. Her Valentine's Day gift boxes were inspired by the cookies that she and her family would bake and give to each other in her childhood. One of her most popular mail-order products is a box of dough—along with cookie cutters—that she markets to mothers who want to make fresh cookies but don't have time to start from scratch. The most honored award one of Cheryl's employees can win is the Elsie Krueger Award, given each year in honor of the grandmother who inspired Cheryl's cookie empire.

There is a little of "us" and "them" at Cheryl's. All the employees park where they like in the same parking lot and use the same cafeteria. There is little distinction between the "executives" and the people who work in the plant making cookies and cakes. Cheryl recalls helping load trucks during a busy Christmas season when she was eight months pregnant. Her employees have no union and seem to have no interest in one.

One of Cheryl's most colorful and most successful employees is a star saleswoman named Cindy Dalton. "I grew up on the East Side of Columbus," Cindy told me. "Almost everybody I knew in those days is dead or in jail or on welfare or on drugs or has a million kids. I was lucky. My first job was as a cook in an Italian restaurant. Cheryl would come in and bring us cookies. She claimed she was going to open a cookie company. We thought she was crazy but we loved her cookies."

Cindy left the Italian restaurant and went to work for J. C. Penney, but she knew she had no future there because she hadn't attended college. One day she received a call from a friend who had gone to work for Cheryl: would she like to come sell cookies over the telephone?

"I thought it was crazy but I decided to try it. I started on May 1, 1989, at $18,500 plus a commission. I was supposed to call companies cold and sell them cookies. I could see we needed bigger sales but I didn't know what the big companies were and you couldn't tell from the phone book. So I drove around town and wrote down the names of the biggest buildings I saw so I could call them."

After only a week with the company, Cindy called Lennox Industries, a cooling and heating company, and asked if they'd like to buy gift baskets to give their employees for Christmas. To her amazement, the person she talked to agreed to buy 1200 gift boxes at $30 each. It was the biggest sale Cheryl's Cookies had ever made. And not long thereafter Cindy sold Midway Airlines 2500 gift tins.

Last year Cindy sold $1.7 million worth of cookies and gifts and, thanks to her commission, made more money than Cheryl. But her job means more to Cindy than money. Before she came to Cheryl's, she says, she and her husband drank far too much. Soon after she started her job, her husband died suddenly, and she thinks she would have fallen apart without Cheryl's support. Today she is thriving because another woman gave her a chance to make the most of herself.

"I'm loyal to this company," Cindy says. "Cheryl said to me, 'I believe you can do this job—you can borrow our belief in you'—and no one else ever said that to me."

Cheryl says: "Our philosophy is to help people achieve their dreams and to help them achieve things they didn't think were possible."

One of Cheryl's first employees, Lisa Henry, had been her assistant at The Limited. She joined Cheryl's Cookies in May 1982, for less money, to handle the paperwork and manage the office. She feared she would never advance at The Limited because she had only one year of college. Today, she's the vice-president in charge of Cheryl's huge catalog sales division.

Cheryl sees no conflict between her family-friendly policies and the pursuit of profits. If you treat your employees well, she thinks, they will repay you with loyalty and hard work and that translates into productivity and profits. In any event, profits have never been Cheryl's greatest goal.

She tries to contribute to the community as well. She operates the Caryl Walker Scholarship Fund to support education. Children from area foster homes are invited to her plant on the annual Take Your Child to Work Day. Her employees are given time off to volunteer at the local Big Brothers-Big Sisters program. Her company participates in Westerville's Adopt a School program and her employees are mentors to underprivileged children. She supports a program in which 4-H Club members sell her cookies and keep part of the profits for their program. Cheryl speaks widely, often to students' and women's groups—usually for free—contributes to a score of local and national charities, and in 1997 donated 1.6 million cookies (that's 167,492 pounds of cookies) to the Mid-Ohio FoodBank to be distributed to homeless shelters, soup kitchens and after-school programs.

Cheryl has created jobs, treated her employees generously and made a contribution to the community at large. You might think, then, that government and the business community would have encouraged this remarkable businesswoman. But that is not the case. She has had to fight every step of the way against prejudice directed at her as a woman, and against the government overregulation that plagues small business owners of both sexes.

As a woman, she was repeatedly denied loans that would have routinely gone to a man with the same assets and credentials. In one case, she was refused a million-dollar loan she needed for expansion until she took a man as a partner. He put up nothing but his name, received a sizable amount of stock, and it later cost her $250,000 to buy him out.

Cheryl married in the 1980s and gave birth to a son, Cavin. The marriage ended in divorce but she and her ex-husband remain friends and partners in raising their son. To her amazement, when she told her bank she was divorcing, the bank informed her it was canceling her $3 million line of credit. "Nothing had changed except I was divorced," Cheryl said. "The president of the bank was someone who said that women don't belong in business. It worked out all right, though. We got a new bank and a better interest rate. But we could have been put out of business. How can they do something like that? We could have sued, but you don't want to get a reputation for suing banks."

More recently, one of her banks announced that it was ending her $3 million line of credit. This came after a worse than average year had been followed by the best year in her company's history. She says the banker told her, "We can't get past your history," meaning the bad year, and she replied, "You can't get past our history or you can't get past our ownership?" She didn't get an answer and she is convinced the bank acted out of prejudice against a woman-owned business. (She adds, however, that there are plenty of other banks that are more than willing to advance her credit.)

One of her many conflicts with state officials concerned her "white chocolate chip" cookies. Strictly speaking, there is no such thing as a "white chocolate chip" cookie. The white chips are cocoa butter. But cookie makers have been selling "white chocolate chip" cookies for years. The state of Ohio told Cheryl she would have to call hers "white confectionary" cookies or "white chip" cookies. She spent tens of thousands of dollars in legal fees before she gave up the battle. What angers her is that other cookie makers still sell "white chocolate chip" cookies but she cannot—nor can she get the state to explain why.

"I don't care what we call them," she says, "as long as the same rules apply to everybody. As it is, your customers wonder what's wrong with you, why you had to change the name of your product."

Once she hired a male executive, only to find that he didn't fit in with her style of management or with her employees. After a year and a half, and several complaints, Cheryl fired the man, only to have him sue her for wrongful dismissal. Her lawyers said she could win the case but it would cost her up to $100,000 in legal fees. Instead, she settled and paid the man $45,000 to be rid of him.

Recently a man who claimed to have found a hair in

one of her cookies sued for $3000 damages for his "mental stress." Another time a girl who ate one of Cheryl's cookies became sick because she was allergic to walnuts. The fact that the package clearly stated that the cookies contained walnuts proved to be no defense and the suit cost her $5000. "These lawsuits are just amazing," she says. "The law should require that the losers pay the winners' legal fees and court costs. If it did, eighty percent of these lawsuits would go away. At what point does the consumer have some responsibility? Most of our customers are great, but there are some that make a business out of these lawsuits."

Like many other small business owners, Cheryl is monumentally frustrated by her dealings with the federal Occupational Safety and Health Administration, or OSHA. It can shut you down, she says, but its rules are incomprehensible and she has to pay a consultant—a former OSHA employee—$2500 a month to try to explain them to her.

More recently, the state has said she has to pay her employees for the fifteen minutes it takes them to change into their uniforms when they report to work. "That can cost us $150,000 a year," she protests. "We don't understand it. Other companies don't pay their employees to change clothes. All we ask is a level playing field." Another time, state inspectors told Cheryl that the display cases in her retail outlets had to have sliding glass doors to protect the cookies. "All those doors do is pinch our employees' fingers," she says. "It costs us a thousand dollars each to install them, then the employees only use them when the inspector comes—and other companies do the same thing."

Cheryl says of the regulators and their rules: "It picks away at you. At what point is there no more incentive to perform?" She adds, "I just wish we could take some of this money we spend on lawyers and on trying to figure out OSHA and open a child-care center here at the plant. But do you have any idea what the liability insurance costs? It's almost impossible."

Cheryl understands that health, safety and sanitation are important. But, like most small business people, she thinks the bureaucrats are often out of control. They build their empires, and people like Cheryl must fight to stay in business despite their endless and often pointless rules. Cheryl, like other small business owners, takes great financial risks to stay in business, knowing that she could lose everything; these risk-takers need to be encouraged by government, not harassed, nitpicked, and overregulated to death.

I think we should pin a medal on Cheryl Krueger, and others like her, not impede and harass them. Cheryl has created hundreds of jobs where none existed before. She pays taxes on her profits. Her policies toward her employees, particularly women like Cindy Dalton and Lisa Henry, could be a model for businesses everywhere. She has been a good citizen, sharing her success and good fortune with the community. We need thousands more business owners with her courage, creativity, compassion and sense of civic duty. It is because of those qualities that she has earned a place among my heroes.

Something Had to Be Done

Gretchen Buchenholz

I had known Gretchen Buchenholz less than five minutes before she asked me to hold a baby. I hesitated, not having much experience with babies, but then the child opened her arms to me and melted my resistance. "She's asking for you," Gretchen said. When I commented on how small she was, Gretchen explained that AIDS babies are smaller than healthy babies. I held the baby for a while, without disaster, then handed her back. I wish I could describe what happened then. There is a radiance that fills Gretchen's face when she holds a child that is unlike anything I have ever seen. It is the beauty of pure love. For more than twenty years this remarkable woman has transformed that love into action on behalf of the most vulnerable children in our society.

GRETCHEN BUCHENHOLZ calls herself "a true New Yorker." She grew up in New York, attended Hunter College and Columbia University there, and in 1974 was teaching sociology at Hunter College and raising a family. Then a problem arose. "I couldn't find a good integrated school for my third child, and I wanted that," she says. "So I founded Merricat's. I only planned to do it for a year but it just grew."

Merricat's Castle Nursery started out in one room that Gretchen rented in the beautiful old Church of the Holy Trinity on East 88th Street on New York's Upper East Side. From the first, Gretchen made sure the nursery was integrated both racially and economically. Some children came from families that could afford to pay several thousand dollars a year tuition; other families paid little or nothing.

In the next few years she noticed how often people came to the church asking for food. Sometimes they made their way to her nursery class as they looked for help. Gretchen responded by starting a pantry program at the church to distribute food, only to be shocked to see "families eating a chicken raw because they had no place to take it home and cook. That's when I realized how many homeless children there were. I was ignorant."

Gretchen met with community groups and prodded the city to make meals for hungry and homeless people in the cafeteria of a nearby public school. "It made sense," she says. "They already had the cooks and the kitchen. They just needed to make extra meals that we could give people after school. It was the least expensive way to feed people." The program started out at the nearby public school and in time spread citywide.

In August 1984, Gretchen went downtown to Church Street, near City Hall, to see a city official. By mistake she walked into the wrong building and found herself in the office where homeless people waited for shelter. What she found there shocked and outraged her. "People were living there, sleeping on the floor, begging for food. There were no Pampers, and four babies in one crib, lying in each other's waste."

The first thing Gretchen did was rush to the nearest store and spend all the money she had on her (she didn't have a credit card then) on bread, peanut butter, juice, Pampers and other necessities, and take them back to the center. Next, she made three phone calls. First she called the deputy mayor, whose office was just across the street, and told him there were hungry children there and he had to feed them. He did nothing. Her second call was to the Red Cross, asking for help. Her third call was to the *New York Times*, which sent a reporter and photographer and the next day carried a story and picture ("On page B1," Gretchen recalls). The *Times* story inspired other reporters to come around.

Seeing those hungry, homeless children made Gretchen think hard about poverty in her hometown, and particularly about the children of poverty. "I began to think this had to be changed. Something had to be done. I wanted to think of alternatives."

She was, of course, just one woman, with little money and no political power—only the power of her outrage, her concern, her determination. But she was right: it was a moment when something had to be done. The crack epidemic was devastating New York. Addicts were not only robbing and killing, they were abusing and abandoning their children at record rates. As a result, there were more and more homeless children, some with a parent, some entirely on their own.

The city had responded to this crisis with "welfare hotels" that were supposed to provide "temporary" shelter to homeless people. Gretchen thought this "solution" was an outrage. The hotels were scandalously expensive. The city would pay as much as $1800 a month for one small, dingy room for a homeless family. The hotel owners were getting rich, the taxpayers were being robbed, and the homeless people were being crammed into dirty, dangerous, often roach- and rat-infested rooms where, Gretchen passionately believed, "no child should be."

Determined to take action, Gretchen and her friend Tom Styron started the Association to Benefit Children (ABC) in 1986. Their first goal was to create a program that would be an alternative to the welfare hotels—one that showed it was possible to provide decent housing at a reasonable cost. She and Styron set out on foot through Harlem looking for a building. It was a voyage of discovery. They encountered drug dealers and addicts, and families living in abandoned buildings without heat or water. In time, they found a five–story, abandoned building on East 124th Street that suited their needs. With the help of a sympathetic city official, David Saltzman, they got a bank loan that enabled them to buy and restore the building, which they now own outright. Rosie and Harry's Place, as they named the center, opened in 1987 and is still in operation today, providing thirteen homeless families with three-bedroom apartments, while a housing team helps them find permanent homes.

With Rosie and Harry's Place under way, Gretchen also started a day care center in an infamous New York welfare hotel, the Martinique. The idea behind it was that, if children had to live in such a dirty, dangerous environment, they should at least have a safe, loving place to spend their days. They didn't reckon with the crack dealers, who didn't like having outsiders on their turf: the day care center was firebombed three separate times.

Gretchen soon seized upon another problem. Because of the crack epidemic, thousands of children, tested soon after birth, were being found to have crack cocaine in their systems. Many suffered serious physical damage because of their mothers' drug use. They and other at–risk children were kept in hospitals until foster homes could be found for them. The problem was that the system was overwhelmed and children were staying weeks, months, even years in hospitals before homes were found. "Boarder babies," they were called. Keeping them in hospitals like that was called "warehousing."

Visiting these hospitals, Gretchen was shocked by what she found. As with the welfare hotels, the city was using the most expensive means possible to care for the children: a foster home would cost a fraction of what hospital care cost. Even worse was the impact a long period of isolation would have on a child at that formative period in its life.

"It was horrible," Gretchen recalls. "When babies were big enough to stand up, they would put tops on the cribs, make them into cages. A healthy baby, treated like that, would never learn to trust or love anyone. They would lose the capacity. It was hard for the bureaucracy to change. They didn't understand the crack epidemic. They would leave babies in hospitals and think they had solved the problem. No one cared. These were babies with no names. They didn't count."

Gretchen's solution was to bring a series of lawsuits against city and state officials, demanding that they move faster to get "warehoused" children out of hospitals and into foster homes. Her passion moved some of the city's best law firms to take the cases *pro bono*.

The pressure of Gretchen's lawsuits resulted in out-of-court settlements in which city and state officials agreed to accelerate the placement of children in foster homes, by speeding up the approval process for foster parents and increasing the fees they are paid. Separate settlements dealt with healthy babies and hard-to-place babies with AIDS or other disabilities. Soon, the city had made dramatic progress in reducing the time taken to place children—down to an average of three days, even for "at-risk" babies. Gretchen's success in New York prompted her to file other lawsuits on behalf of boarder babies in New Jersey and elsewhere.

Gretchen also launched a series of lawsuits intended to protect the lives of babies born with AIDS. In New York, every newborn baby was tested for HIV infection. The problem was that these were "blind" tests. State officials knew how many infected babies were being born, but no one—not a child's mother, doctor, or foster parents—was told if a particular child was HIV positive. Why? As columnist Nat Hentoff put it, in a column that praised Gretchen's crusade: "Gay rights groups and women's activists have transformed AIDS testing into a near religious crusade. The unbending dogma holds that nothing shall call into doubt the privacy of adults with AIDS—even if infants are condemned to short, painful lives."

There was a time when early diagnosis of HIV infection made no difference for children, because there were no effective treatments for the disease. But by the mid-1990s there were effective treatments, and not to divulge the information was to condemn hundreds of children to death. Gretchen's lawsuits forced state and city officials to divulge the information that would make that treatment possible. In 1995, state officials agreed to divulge HIV data on children in foster care—the ones over whom they have direct control. The state also agreed to divulge HIV data to the mothers of newborns; the mothers could then seek treatment for themselves and their children.

Even as ABC was filing these lawsuits, it was expanding its programs to help children and families. Today, ABC operates nearly a dozen programs that help children and families in need. Three of them are located within a few blocks of each other on the Upper East Side.

Cassidy's Place, the newest of the three, is a therapeutic center that serves, free of charge, about a hundred poor, terminally ill children, many with AIDS and cancer, and their families. The center has eight classrooms where young teachers and volunteers operate day care classes for some of the city's most medically endangered children, with special emphasis on those age five and under.

In one classroom I visited, volunteers played with two small brothers. One boy kept singing "Happy Birthday" over and over. Then he gave his brother a "birthday cake" made of a piece of clay with a twig stuck in it for a candle. Both boys, Gretchen explained, had been severely abused by their parents. When they were brought to her, they were dirty, starving and unloved. No one had taught them to laugh or ever sung to them. The younger one was barely responsive to the playfulness of his brother and the attempts of the volunteers to engage him. These are the children to whom Gretchen has dedicated her life.

Gretchen is quick to deflect praise from herself. She says of her young teachers: "Our teachers are heroic. After the first child, they understand that these kids they give all their love to are going to die. But they don't hold back on their love, even though they know they'll suffer terrible pain and loss. That's the most marvelous thing about this work, that people have that kind of love in them."

Merricat's preschool day nursery program integrates homeless, handicapped and terminally ill children with healthy children from the neighborhood whose parents can afford to pay tuition of more than $10,000 a year. (There is a waiting list of parents who are able and willing to pay that amount.) About a third of the children are ill or handicapped, and there are special health, education and psychological programs for them and their families. Gretchen considers Merricat's the cornerstone of all ABC's programs—a national model for "inclusive" preschool programs.

Finally, on 91st Street, Gretchen started Variety Cody Gifford House for Children with Special Needs. Like Cassidy's Place, it is named for one of the children of Frank and Kathy Lee Gifford, who have been major contributors to ABC. Variety House offers foster care, adoption and therapeutic programs for children who are homeless and/or have severe handicaps or serious medical problems. The program works to find and train a loving family to care for each child.

What I remember most about Variety House, however, is the playground out back. Working *pro bono*, landscape architect Christina Maile and architect Nasser Ahari created a mountainside seating area, a lawn flanked with brick paths, and a play area complete with climbing equipment and a wooden elephant and giraffes, all in just 1200 square feet. The brick wall of the building next door makes up one side of the playground. On that wall, young people have painted a huge mural that is a kind of city child's fantasy of another, safer world. There are green fields and flowing streams, sheep and rabbits, castles floating in the air, and many pigeons flying over the landscape—"a city bird," Gretchen explained.

I noticed that some of the pigeons had names and dates written across their white, feathery breasts.

"A boy named Wilfredo lived here while he was dying," Gretchen explained. "His mother had already died of AIDS. He was a lovely boy. After he died, his father asked if we could bury him here in the playground. I said we couldn't but we would build a memorial to him. But I didn't know how. Then someone had the idea of putting his name and dates on one of the pigeons. After that, we did it for other children who died. It's a wonderful image of flying upward, above the earth, free of all pain. We think of this as holy ground."

The day I visited was cold and gray, and a light rain was falling. Gretchen choked back tears as she spoke. I studied the names and dates above us: "Wilfredo, 3-19-88–9-15-91." And the others: Franklin, Lisa, Brandon, Kenny, Sean, ten names in all. Gretchen was right: this was holy ground. And this remarkable woman, because of her love for children, had made it all happen.

Schools
on Wheels

Agnes Stevens

When I was growing up, I knew many Catholic nuns at the church I attended, and I came to think that they are amazing human beings. Those determined women make great sacrifices for their faith, giving up marriage and children to meet the challenge of putting the Bible's teachings into action. Agnes Stevens is a nun through and through, even though she left her order. She is highly principled, and when she makes up her mind she acts without regard to the consequences. She truly has the courage of her convictions.

WHEN AGNES STEVENS was a child, during the Great Depression years of the late 1930s, her family often moved from town to town as her father looked for work. Born in Boston, the youngest of five children, she remembers living in Connecticut, Rhode Island, and several towns in upstate New York. Once the family moved five times in one year and wound up in a cheap hotel. Those memories, she thinks, are part of the reason that, a half century later, she feels such compassion for the homeless children she serves with her program, Schools on Wheels, in the Los Angeles area.

Agnes calls her mother, a strong woman and a strict Catholic, the greatest influence on her childhood. "My mother taught me to laugh and to survive," Agnes says. In addition to Agnes, three of her four siblings entered the Catholic Church. Both Agnes and her older sister became nuns—and later left the order. One of her brothers became a Jesuit priest, but he also left. Another of her brothers, William, became an Irish Christian Brother, and today is working with AIDS patients in New Jersey.

At sixty-one, Agnes is a pleasant, sturdy woman whose gray hair is curly and close-cropped. She is a strong-minded idealist who single-handedly, in less than four years, built Schools on Wheels from a program with one volunteer tutor to a program with more than two hundred tutors. Agnes has little talent for administration or fund

raising—little interest in them, really—but she is a determined, charismatic leader who can move others to action.
Almost no one can say no to her, because her only motivation is so clearly to help others.

She wasn't always like that. As a shy young nun, still
in her teens, she was assigned to fund raising and she can
remember how her hands shook whenever she got up to
speak. Fortunately, her superiors sent her to college to
study to be a teacher and she found that she loved teaching. Her first assignment was teaching Chinese and Italian
kids in a parochial school in New York's Greenwich Village. From there, she was sent to Chicago to teach in a
Chinese neighborhood. Finally she was told that she would
be sent to Los Angeles. "I cried," Agnes remembers. "I
didn't want to go to California."

She arrived in Los Angeles in 1963, lived in a housing
project and taught mostly Japanese children. She also
found herself questioning the Church. "This was the
1960s," she recalls. "Times were changing but the Church
wasn't moving. I was restless."

In 1969 she left the Church and got a job teaching in
a public school in Pico Rivera, a community south of Los
Angeles.

Later, after a marriage of thirteen years, she taught for
about six months in another Catholic school but left because she thought the school administrators were too interested in their bureaucracy and too little interested in
teaching. It was at that school that she assigned a student
to write an essay and he used every four–letter word in the
book to tell her how much he hated her. Agnes took the
insults in stride and gave the student an A minus because
he had made his message clear. "Expand your vocabulary
and you might be something," she told the boy, who became her best student.

In 1985, Agnes read a book about homeless families in New York City that made a powerful impression on her. "It was the first time I realized there were homeless *families*," she says. "You saw homeless men, but families were more hidden, because they were afraid their children would be taken away from them. I began to think I would work with homeless families when I retired from teaching."

In May 1989, Agnes did retire, and used all her savings to make the down payment on a mobile home in Paradise Cove, a mobile home community in Malibu. A short walk from her door, she can glimpse the Pacific Ocean. That ocean view is all she ever sought for herself. To help pay her mortgage, she began to tutor. Some of the children she taught were the sons and daughters of the movie stars who live in and near Malibu.

The plight of the homeless still haunted her. She worried in particular about the children. As they moved from place to place, they might not attend school at all, or if they did their education might have huge gaps. Yet if they were not educated, what chance would they have of ever escaping poverty?

She spoke with school officials and with the operator of one homeless shelter, who told her that education for homeless children was not a problem. She knew better. In 1990 she found a public school in Venice that had a special program to help children who were at risk, including homeless children. As many as a quarter of the school's students were homeless or living in shelters or cars. She began volunteering at the school two days a week. A turning point came one Friday when she met two brothers, a sixth grader and a fourth grader, both of whom told her they'd never learned to read because they'd been traveling around the country with their grandmother.

Agnes thought about the brothers all weekend—but on Monday, when she sent for them, they were gone.

"That really affected me," Agnes recalls. "I thought, 'What can be done?' I started writing things down." She began to imagine a program that would seek out homeless children—go to them, wherever they were—and tutor them one on one and help them get enrolled in school. She soon thought up a name for her program: Schools on Wheels. Even if it sounded a lot like Meals on Wheels, she thought it was catchy and people would remember it.

A lawyer friend, Richard Scott, advised her to incorporate as a nonprofit organization, so she could raise money and not have to pay taxes on it, and she got her incorporation papers in April 1993. Not long after that Agnes and a friend went to Memorial Park in Santa Monica and found a homeless girl of five or so. They made friends with her and began to teach her, the three of them sitting on a park bench. "Her mother was thrilled," Agnes says. "She brought another homeless family with three kids. Others began to come. We had no materials, except paper and pencils, but we found people to help. By the end of the summer we had four or five tutors and were working with a shelter."

Agnes sought out homeless children, in shelters, in cheap motels, even those who lived with their parents in their cars. She decided she needed an office so potential contributors would take her seriously, and she persuaded a skeptical businessman to rent her one at half price. She went to people she knew, often to the parents of children she had tutored, in search of money and volunteers. Money for rent, gasoline and other expenses was always a problem. She found out that some television studios would pay groups to be in the audience when they taped their programs, and for a while she raised money by organizing friends who were willing to laugh at nutty sitcoms. She started an 800-number hotline for homeless families to call. Word of her program began to spread. The Malibu paper carried a story. An ad in the *Los Angeles Times* brought in more than a hundred calls from potential volunteers. She recruited students from nearby Pepperdine College.

"At first we didn't know who the tutors would be," she says. "They turned out to be mostly professionals. Lawyers, engineers, students, people in the movie industry. You have to have a generosity of spirit. You have to understand that, just as you get attached to a child, that child may move away and you never see it again. Sometimes the parents call us from other states, to say they're doing better and the kids are in school. Our tutors are young and old, black and white, liberal and conservative. The thing I'm proudest of is that we have no agenda except education."

Agnes is thrilled that when people get back on their feet they often call and thank her and Schools on Wheels. Those calls are part of what keeps her going.

I asked Agnes who the homeless were.

"I think there are three main groups," she said. "The first are those who are homeless because of the economy or illness. They lose their jobs, use up all their savings, can't afford rent and find themselves on the street. In the past, maybe they would have moved in with family, but there's less family structure today. Once, your Uncle Joe or your friends would help you. But the breakdown of the family has all too often left us isolated.

"The second group are mothers who are escaping physical abuse. They now know that not only do they suffer but their children are being scarred. They have the courage to leave their husbands but often have no place to go. Third are what I call the dark side, people with drug and alcohol problems or mental problems."

I asked Agnes if she is ever shocked by what she sees.

"I cry every four or five months," she said. "I'll see these children who are adrift, who have nothing, and it hits me, they're so lost and helpless."

One hot Friday in August 1997, Agnes and her friend Nita Rodriguez took me to one of the shelters where their tutors work with homeless children. When Agnes started the program in 1993, she worked in two shelters in Santa Monica and Venice. By 1997 her volunteers were working in eleven shelters in eight communities in and around Los Angeles.

The shelter we visited, the Sunshine Mission Church, on Fourteenth Street in Santa Monica, is headed by a colorful individual who was born Harold Feldman but for many years has been known as Pastor Kenny. As a young man he pursued a singing career, but when he married a Christian woman he converted from Judaism to Christianity and he and his wife decided to open a mission. That was more than forty years ago. His Sunshine Mission provides beds for a hundred people, and usually about half of them are children. The living accommodations at the shelter are minimal, so that as many people as possible can be squeezed in. Entire families live in rooms not much bigger than a closet, often separated from other families only by a curtain. One of the tutors told me it took her six months before she could stand to go upstairs and see where her child lived.

Pastor Kenny and his family and volunteers serve four meals a day—"We want the kids to have a snack at night," he explains—and let people stay nine or ten months, to give them a chance to get back on their feet. He accepts no government money, and once turned down $30,000 in federal funds because he doesn't want anyone telling him how to run his program. "We give people food and clothing and shelter," Pastor Kenny says, "but that doesn't solve the problem. They need to turn to God. A lot of people have come here and accepted Christ and gone on to very successful lives."

I talked with Chris and Karen, who have been married for twelve years and have been living at the Sunshine Mission for more than a year. Chris is forty-seven and has a full brown beard. Karen is an attractive, soft-spoken woman with long brown hair. They have two daughters, aged nine and eleven, and older children from previous marriages. Chris once had his own business, a telephone answering service, but both of them became addicted to drugs—"Every drug you can imagine," Chris says—and they lost everything.

"For a long time Chris would say, 'I don't have a drug problem—I *like* drugs,' " Karen told me. "Now my sixteen-year-old son has been experimenting with marijuana. It scares me. He says it won't lead to anything else. I tell him, 'That's what I thought.' "

When I met Karen, she was working part time at Toys Я Us and Chris had become the shelter's resident handyman. "I can fix things with my hands," he says. Both of them are off drugs and they have turned to Christianity. "For a long time I had my life ninety percent under control," Chris says, "but could never fix that last ten percent. But now we have God on our side. We've let God into our lives." Recently Pastor Kenny agreed that Chris could build an apartment for himself and his family at the back of the shelter. The new apartment will be bigger and more comfortable than their crowded accommodations upstairs. Chris believes this new apartment came in answer to his prayers.

Valerie Cavanaugh, a lawyer who recently retired after a successful career in television, is tutoring Chris and Karen's older daughter, Chanel, who is eleven. Valerie and her husband do not have children and she has gained great pleasure and satisfaction from tutoring Chanel.

"Homeless kids in the public schools are always behind," she says. "They're always the new kids. They're shy. They change schools all the time and they miss things. One-on-one tutoring is exactly what they need. I tutored a girl named Ruby who was failing eighth-grade social studies, even though she read extremely well. Agnes figured out that she had poor study skills. She hadn't learned to read the boldface questions at the end of each chapter—*because those are the questions that will be on the exams.* We got her up to a C, then her mother got a job and she changed schools. We found out that her new social studies class was five weeks behind the old one. We told her, *'Don't tell them!* Just raise your hand a lot and answer the questions.' Pretty soon she was making a B.

"You lose these kids. I tutored a boy named Carlos who couldn't read. I followed him from shelters to apartments. The family was intact. My husband gave Carlos's father a job—but he went back on drugs and lost the job. The mother took the children back to Detroit. She sent me a note and said they're doing okay. You stay with them as long as you can."

Valerie heard about Schools on Wheels after it started. "My friend and I drove out to Agnes's dingy little office in Malibu. I told her, 'I'm not a teacher.' Agnes said, 'I'll train you—you can read, right?' She's really gifted. This program has a real, live beating heart—and it's Agnes. You may think she's disorganized, but she focuses on kids and is wonderful with them. She understands their strengths and weaknesses. She gave me books and flash cards. It turns out almost anyone can teach with a little guidance.

"In television, almost everyone I know does flashy charities where they have big dinners to raise money. That doesn't seem as meaningful to me as working directly with the kids. I find it incredibly gratifying. This is a wonderful organization and it's all Agnes. As my Irish grandmother used to say, she's a saint walking."

Valerie tutored Chanel through the fifth grade. She thinks of Chuck and Karen as middle-class people who've been unlucky and she thinks their two daughters can survive the ordeal of homelessness and go on to productive lives. "Chanel is a really good kid and a good student." she says. "She's an oldest child, so she really wants to do well—her younger sister, Onalise, is more of a free spirit. In the fifth grade, Chanel was student of the month twice—I was so proud of that. She wrote a paper on George Washington that got the best grade in the class. She's very good at math—better than I am—but she didn't know the multiplication tables. She'd somehow missed them. So this summer I started a special program for Chanel, Onalise and three of their friends. I wanted to teach them water coloring, but I have a theory that you can do two things at the same time. In TV, I found I could talk on the phone and do paperwork too. So in this class we paint water colors and recite the multiplication tables at the same time. And it worked."

For Valerie, Schools on Wheels has opened up a new, immensely rewarding life. Now that she has retired, she plans to tutor not only Chanel but at least two other children, commuting from her comfortable home in Brentwood to the Sunshine Mission. She doesn't want to raise money for Schools on Wheels, she says—although she knows the program desperately needs money—because her joy comes from working directly with the children.

Another of the tutors, Barbara Botos, works for British Airways and is one of Agnes's neighbors in the mobile home park. Barbara tutors Chanel's younger sister, Onalise, and she is enthusiastic about the girl's potential. "Agnes was talking about this program in my living room for years before it started," Barbara told me. "I'm not a teacher, but Agnes told me, 'Just teach what you know.' It's very rewarding. Instead of just dropping money in a collection box and not knowing where it goes, I see the people I help. The children look forward to your coming and you can see them make progress. But it hurts when you become attached to them and they leave. Agnes is very special. She had a dream and she stuck with it."

The help that tutors like Valerie Cavanaugh and Barbara Botos give is psychological as well as educational. To children thrust into the chaos of homelessness, it means a lot to have some continuity in their lives, to have a caring adult come and help them every week. Agnes insists on one-on-one tutoring so each child will feel a special bond with the tutor.

"Sometimes we can give the kids backpacks loaded with school supplies," Agnes says. "Those kids are so proud of their backpacks that they pop their buttons."

Many people dream of wealth or fame or a comfortable retirement, but Agnes dreams of having Schools on Wheels working in dozens, even hundreds more homeless shelters in every part of California and across the United States. She can hardly sit still as she explains the challenge that awaits her. "And then Oakland!" she declares with a big grin. If you know Agnes, you can't doubt that she is happier in her trailer than many of her Malibu neighbors are in their million-dollar mansions.

Agnes Stevens

In her dream, she would "franchise" the program. In other cities, the organizers could use the Schools on Wheels name to attract volunteers, and she would provide the experience and instructional materials to get them started. In the meantime it is a struggle to keep the program growing. Money is always a problem. Agnes estimates that the program spends about $3000 a month on her salary (which the board of directors recently raised to $1500 a month), the salary of one part time office worker, rent, phones, gas, school supplies and backpacks for the kids, and other expenses. If she had another one or two thousand dollars a month, she would use it to pay someone to help with the administration of the program, so she could spend more time seeking volunteers and money. She hopes to receive foundation grants, but it is only now, after her program has spent several years proving its merit, that foundations will consider helping.

Knowing Agnes, I have no doubt that she will find more money to enable Schools on Wheels to grow. She combines idealism with tenacity and that is a hard combination to beat.

When I parted from Agnes and her friend Nita Rodriguez, Nita said, "If each one would help one, there's no end to what we could do." Each one help one. In an America too often divided between haves and have-nots, that could be a motto for us all.

A Whisper
from Above

Irene Gut Opdyke

*As a Polish Catholic teenager, Irene Gut Opdyke
exhibited incredible courage as she confronted
the evil of the Nazis face to face, repeatedly risk-
ing her life to save the lives of Jews. How did a
teenage girl summon such courage? "Courage is
a whisper from above," she told me when I
visited her home in California. Irene's wartime
heroism took place many years ago, in another
country, but her courage is still relevant
today—it is eternal, and it continues to inspire
the young people she talks to all over America.*

IN SEPTEMBER 1939, Irene Gut was a seventeen-year-old nursing student in the Polish town of Radom, separated from her home and family for the first time. The oldest of five daughters of an architect, Irene had enjoyed an idyllic childhood, but her carefree life was soon to end. Her beloved Poland was trapped between two relentless enemies, the Russians to the east and the Germans to the west. That September, when the first bombs fell on Radom, she and many other students fled into the nearby forest. But winter soon came, bitter cold, and one day she ventured back into the town in search of food and clothing. There the slender, golden-haired, beautiful young woman was seized by Russian soldiers who brutally beat and raped her. Nearly sixty years later, she told me sadly that up to that point she had never even kissed a boy.

Someone took her to a hospital where Russian doctors cared for her and, when she was well enough, let her assist them as a nurse. But when one of the doctors tried to force himself upon her, another doctor sent her to live with a woman named Meriam in the village of Swietlana, just across the Russian border, where she lived until early 1941. Eventually she managed to return to Poland, where she was reunited with her family and lived with her aunt in Radom, near the Russian border.

Soon, however, the Germans took her father to manage a factory near the German border. Her mother decided she must go to care for him. Irene was left in charge of her younger sisters. One Sunday, after church, Irene and other young Poles were rounded up by German soldiers, put in trucks and taken to a barracks. Those who protested were beaten.

Irene was put to work on the assembly line in an ammunition factory in Radom. Frail and sick, one day she passed out. When she woke, she was in the office of the German major who ran the factory. A tall, gaunt man in his late sixties with thinning hair and a lined face, his name was Eduard Rugemer. Impressed by Irene's intelligence and her command of German, he offered her a job serving meals to the German officers and secretarial staff. Moreover, she could live at home, with her Aunt Helen and sister Janina. She eagerly reported for work the next morning at the old hotel where the German officers and secretaries lived and took their meals. Her immediate boss was Herr Schultz, a stout, genial German who spoke no Polish and was delighted to have her as an interpreter. She was even allowed to take leftover food home to her aunt and sister. For months Irene had heard nothing from her parents.

One of Irene's duties was to serve lunch to the German officers in an upstairs dining room. It was a large, elegant room with velvet drapes that covered stately windows. Sometimes, when she was alone there, Irene liked to pull back the drapes and gaze on the world below. What she did not at first understand was that the world she saw was a ghetto. There, as in so many cities, Jewish neighborhoods had been walled in and the inhabitants made prisoners.

One morning in December, Irene was setting the table for lunch when she heard gunfire and screams outside. Alarmed, she pushed back the thick velvet drapes and saw German SS men beating and shooting defenseless men, women and children. Bodies littered the street and the snow was stained with blood.

When Irene started to scream, Herr Schultz rushed in and put his hand over her mouth. If she caused a scene, he warned, the German officers might think she was sympathetic to the Jews. "Terrible things happen to Jew-lovers," he added grimly.

That night Irene discussed these horrors with her aunt and sister. She and her sister recalled the Jewish children who had been their playmates. Her parents had taught her to love and care for others: Germans, Poles, Russians, Jews, all were the same. She and her sisters were taught to help the poor. Needy neighbors were invited for holiday dinners. An empty chair was left at their table during holidays—reserved for God. The cruelty of the Germans was incomprehensible to her.

Angry and confused, she challenged her faith in God. She demanded that God tell her how He could permit such cruelty. Suddenly she experienced an epiphany: She realized that God had given humans free will, to choose good or evil. She prayed to God for forgiveness and asked only for an opportunity to help. Her faith restored, she resolved to help the Jews in any way she could.

With her sister's help, Irene gathered leftover food from the hotel and put it in a jar. When no one was watching, she slipped the jar through the fence that surrounded the ghetto. The next day, she found the jar where she had left it, but empty. She continued to pass the food to unknown Jews throughout the winter. One day at the end of March, when Irene reported for work, she found the fence around the ghetto down; bulldozers were destroying the houses, and the people were gone.

Major Rugemer asked Irene to prepare a special diet for him, because he had ulcers. As she got to know him better, she learned that he was a widower and was managing the factory because of his job skills, not because he was a committed Nazi. When the German advance into Russia began, the major told Irene that they would move their operation east, along with the army, into Tarnopol. Before the move, Irene again witnessed the Germans rounding up Jews, in scenes even worse than the one she had seen from the window. One German officer tore a child from its mother's arm, bashed its head against the sidewalk, and then shot the hysterical mother. An old rabbi was beaten to death with a rifle butt while he said his prayers. Once again, Irene vowed to do everything she could to help the innocent victims.

In August 1942, Irene and Janina arrived at another, bigger ammunition factory in Tarnopol. A fence surrounded the factory, an old hotel, barracks for the soldiers, and other buildings, one of which held a laundry room. Irene and Janina shared a tiny room off the kitchen in the hotel where officers lived. For all their suffering and uncertainty, they at least had food and a warm place to sleep.

Irene learned that she and her sister would be serving meals for about twenty German officers, fifteen secretaries, one hundred and fifty German soldiers, and three hundred Jewish men and women who were brought from a nearby ghetto each day to work in the factory. The SS detail that brought them was directed by a sinister German officer named Rokita, the commander of the local SS.

Along with serving meals, Irene was assigned to supervise the laundry room and the twelve Jews who were assigned to work there. They were educated people—a lawyer, a medical student, an accountant, businessmen and -women—but now they were happy to work in the laundry room, where there were better conditions and they might survive. Irene soon became friends with them and began to smuggle food for them to eat and to take back to their friends in the ghetto.

Irene told the major she needed more help with the housecleaning. Because he was pleased with her work, he authorized her to select more Jews from the ghetto to join the others working in the laundry room.

Rokita, the SS commander, often came to drink and dine with Major Rugemer. When Irene heard Rokita speak of raids to "thin" the ghetto, she told her friends and urged them to hide. Yet many had no place to hide, even if warned. One of the Jews in the laundry room, a lawyer named Lazar Hallar, told her that people in the ghetto were desperately creating hiding places wherever they could. He asked if they might construct a hiding place in the laundry room, where the twelve of them might hide if a raid was coming. She quickly agreed. Shelves covered one wall of the laundry room, and with Irene's help the Jews constructed a false wall, giving them a narrow hiding place behind the shelves.

When Rokita began to make advances to Irene's sister Janina, she helped her flee to their hometown with the approval of the major. When an angry Rokita confronted Irene, she stammered that her sister was sick with tuberculosis.

Early in 1943, as reports circulated of the Germans' disastrous retreat from Stalingrad, the factory began to work extra shifts. In June there were rumors that many of the Jews in the local ghetto would be taken elsewhere to work in the war effort. Irene's friends were terrified. Two of the couples in the laundry room told Irene they planned to flee into a forest some ten kilometers away and pleaded for her help.

Irene had a friend who could borrow a horse and wagon from a farmer. One morning she persuaded Herr

Schultz to give her the day off and drove the two young couples to the forest, hidden under blankets, straw and a bag of potatoes. She left them in the forest, then returned the horse and wagon, with a bottle of vodka and cigarettes for the farmer.

The raids on the ghetto grew worse. One night she overheard Rokita telling the major that all the Jews would soon be "terminated." She was so shaken that she fell to the floor and dropped the tray she was carrying. When she told her Jewish friends what she had heard, they begged her to help them. "I will not let you die if I can help it," she promised.

Around the middle of June the major told Irene he was going to move into a private home a few blocks away from the factory, and she would be his housekeeper. He added ominously that he wanted her to train "a new crew" to work in the laundry.

The major's new house was large, set back from the street, surrounded by trees, and fenced in. It would be a perfect hiding place, if somehow she could get her friends out of the laundry room before the SS seized them. Lazar Hallar told her, "I know that house. It was designed by a Jewish architect. It is rumored that a hiding place was built into it."

Irene warned as many Jews as she could of the coming "termination." She stole a pass from the major's drawer and then rode her bicycle around the town, telling every Jew she saw to flee. On July 15 she heard SS Commander Rokita tell the major: "The twenty-second of July is it. Don't expect any more Jews to come to work. Tarnopol will be *Judenfrei*—free of Jews."

Irene, by then, had seen two faces of evil. The Russians, she thought, were raw, rough and cruel. The Nazis, on the other hand, were clean, mannerly and utterly without emotions or feelings—"murderers in white gloves," she called them. Now the white-gloved murderers were closing in on her friends. When she told her friends what she had heard, they cried and prayed but had no solution. The major's new house, their dreamed-of sanctuary, was still occupied. Finally Irene had an idea.

"Don't go back to the camp the night of the twenty-first," she told them. "Stay here in I'll lock you in the laundry room for the night. The next night the house should be vacant and somehow I'll smuggle you in."

"Irene, we'll be discovered," her friends protested. "They'll take you and us to our deaths. You'll be killed."

"I am in God's hands," the young woman replied. "His will be done."

On the night of the twenty-first her friends hid behind the false wall in the laundry room. The next day Irene watched as Jews in the ghetto were herded up and taken away.

"I trembled as the victims were escorted to waiting trucks," she wrote later. "I will never forget the looks on those people's faces. They knew they faced a death sentence. They were being delivered into Rokita's hands. I had done all I could to help them. Only my prayers could aid them now."

That evening Herr Schultz told her that the SS was coming to search for Jews who might have hidden where they worked. Irene was terrified. She feared the false wall in the laundry room would not survive a close search.

What could she do? Once again this young woman, barely in her twenties, had an inspiration. She noticed a screen on the wall in the major's bathroom, about one and a half meters square, something she had never paid attention to before. Now she stood on a chair and removed the screen. Behind it was an opening, an air vent, about two meters long, with another screen on the other end. Could six people hide overnight in that small space? Yes, she decided, they could if their lives depended on it.

That night most of the Germans went to the theater. Two stayed behind with a cold—Irene prayed that they would sleep soundly. Between ten o'clock and midnight she slipped the six Jews out of the laundry room and up the stairs to the major's bathroom, where one by one they climbed into the air vent. She gave them food and drink, blankets and pillows, then replaced the screen. She knew that one cough, one squeak, could be their undoing, but she was convinced it was a safer hiding place than the laundry room.

She lay sleepless that night. She heard the Germans stagger in drunk around two in the morning. The next day they stumbled down with hangovers. No sooner had they left for work than the Gestapo arrived to search for Jews. As soon as she could, the anxious Irene hurried up to the bathroom, only to find an SS officer coming out of it. He had gone there to relieve himself and left indignantly when Irene expressed surprise at finding him in the major's suite. When he was gone, Irene locked the door and let her friends climb down.

Throughout the day Irene heard more gunshots, screams and explosions as the SS continued to round up those who had no place to hide. Late that night, when the major was asleep, she slipped her six friends out of the hotel and through the dark, quiet streets to the major's new home, where she hid them in the basement.

The next morning Irene suggested to the major that she go to his new home and start to clean it and direct the painters. At the house she found not the six Jews she had guided there the night before, but ten refugees—the six had invited four of their friends to join them. They decided that the safest hiding place would be the small, hot, dusty attic, where the painters would not be working.

"We entered a very difficult time," Irene recalls. "My friends were miserable in the attic. There was no bathroom or running water. It was hard for me to keep taking food and other necessities to them with workers and soldiers all over the place."

When Irene suggested to the major that she move into the new house, to better supervise the work there, he said that was an excellent idea and added that he would also move his orderly into the house. Irene was horrified. There was no way she could keep ten people hidden in the house if an orderly was living there.

"Please don't bring a young man to live in the house," she pleaded.

Suspicious, the major asked her what was wrong. Irene told him about her rape by the Russians, and claimed she could never be comfortable with a young man living in the house. The major accepted her story and dropped the idea.

Irene's friends searched the house for its rumored hiding place and found it in the basement: a narrow tunnel that led to a bunker underneath the gazebo in the garden. The bunker had been built with air vents and was big enough for all those Irene was hiding. They stored food and water there and it became their refuge of last resort.

Soon Irene and her friends developed a routine. They spent the nights locked in the basement storage room. When the major left in the morning, Irene locked the door behind him, then let her friends out to eat, exercise, read newspapers and listen to the war news on the radio. At midmorning Irene would lock them back in the basement and go to the factory to serve lunch. Sometimes the major would return home early, so they had to be ready to retreat to the basement hideaway on a moment's notice. Months went by, with Major Rugemer oblivious to his unseen "guests." Ironically, Irene noticed that the Germans had put up signs all over town saying THIS TOWN IS JEW-FREE!

One day, the major told Irene he was going to have a housewarming to show his new home to a few colleagues, including SS Commander Rokita. As always, Irene insisted that she handle the preparations alone—in fact, the Jews helped her.

Just before the party began, Irene had a premonition of disaster and insisted that her friends retreat to the bunker, in case any of the guests insisted on seeing the basement. There was much drinking that evening and Irene discovered that some of the officers and their ladies had taken refuge in the upstairs bedrooms. Later, when she saw Rokita and his date embracing in the shadowy gazebo in the garden, she quickly made an excuse to interrupt them, and infuriated the disheveled SS officer.

The next morning her friends had a great laugh about the way Irene had interrupted Rokita's love scene—they had heard everything from their hiding place beneath the gazebo.

They had little else to laugh about. Irene's friends—her family, as she had come to think of them—were tired, nervous, and in some cases sick. Many said the only thing that kept them going was their determination that the world must someday know the truth about the Nazi evil.

One day Major Rugemer arrived unexpectedly with some young SS men.

"The very idea!" Irene heard the major declare. "A German officer accused of hiding Jews!"

The flustered SS men stammered that there must have been a mistake, that they did not really need to search his house, but the major angrily insisted that they carry out a complete search. The embarrassed soldiers quickly looked around the house. When they reached the stairs to the basement, a trembling Irene asked if they wanted to look down there.

"No, *Fräulein*, we've seen enough," they stammered, and left with more apologies to the major.

Irene had no idea who had told the SS there were Jews in the major's house, but she realized that all their lives were at risk. Perhaps a delivery man had heard voices or smelled her friends' tobacco smoke. How absurdly careless they had been, she thought. Just a few days later someone left a blackmail note on the porch. "I know you're hiding thirty Jews in the house," it began and went on to demand a large amount of money or the Gestapo would be told.

Irene and her friends debated how to deal with this threat. They finally agreed on the most audacious strategy of all: she turned the blackmail note over to the major. As they had hoped, he called the SS and the blackmailer was arrested. Presumably he paid the price for making such an outrageous charge against a German officer!

In the fall of 1943, Lazar Hallar's wife Ida became pregnant. Others in the group asked Irene to get the equipment they would need for an abortion, but Irene refused. Too many babies had died already, she insisted—this one must live! Lazar and Ida agreed, although clearly they could not hide a baby in the major's house. As Ida's pregnancy advanced, Irene tried to think of a way to save her friends and their child. Irene had met a sympathetic Polish forester, who was helping Jews hiding in the forest, but a newborn child might not survive a winter there.

One day in November 1943, amid talk of a German retreat, Irene was out shopping when SS troops suddenly ordered her and other bystanders to gather in the town square. A scaffold, adorned with nooses, had been erected.

Two families were slowly led to the scaffold by the SS. One was a Polish couple with two small children. The other was a Jewish couple with one child, all three wearing the yellow Star of David. The SS announced their "crime"— the Polish couple had given sanctuary to the Jewish family. As a result, all seven were hanged as Irene and the towns-people watched in silence.

For Irene, the scene was nightmarish. "Innocent people killed for saving lives?" she wrote later. "I saw the same fate ahead for me, if my actions were ever discovered. But I had to go on as before. I had no choice."

When the SS finally let people leave, Irene stumbled back to the major's house in a state of shock. Too dazed to realize what she was doing, she neglected to lock the door behind her. She unlocked the door to the basement, and three of the young women came upstairs to help her in the kitchen. Clara, the nurse, saw that Irene was shaken and asked what was wrong. As Irene was trying to decide whether to tell them of the horror she had witnessed, the front door flew open and the major marched in.

There was no time for the women to flee. The major looked at them and knew in an instant that the "absurd rumors" of Jews in his house were true. He hurried into his library and seized the telephone.

Irene ran after him, persuaded him to put down the phone, and tearfully pleaded for her friends' lives.

"Irene, you know what I must do," he shouted. "You know the punishment for this!"

"Yes, *Herr* Major," the young woman replied boldly. "This morning I was forced to witness a Polish family being hanged in the marketplace, just because they tried to help other human beings. Nobody has the right to kill an-other human being because of race or religion!"

She pleaded with the major to spare her friends. She

told him he was a good man, a decent man, not like the others, and he must show mercy.

"You deceived me," he said angrily. "How could you do it? I believed in you. I gave you a home and you have deceived me!"

"Punish me but let them go!" Irene cried.

The major began to waver. "I'm old and tired," he said. "Tired of the war and tired of killing."

Finally he said he must go to his office and he would announce his decision later.

Once he had left, Irene told her friends what had happened. Should they flee? they asked. No, she told them, they would only be picked up by the SS. Better to hide under the gazebo and await the major's decision. If she was taken away and did not return, then they must flee.

When the major returned that night he was drunk. Irene went to him and he pulled her onto his lap; as he fumbled with her blouse he announced his decision. He would keep her secret, spare her and her friends, but there was a price: she must become his mistress.

Irene saw at once that she had no choice. If the price of saving many lives was to sleep with this tired old man, she must pay it.

Christmas came and went. The Russians were drawing closer. The major must not have been discreet, because Herr Schultz told Irene there were rumors of the affair. But her friends were safe. Ida grew close to the day her child would arrive. In February 1944 the major told Irene that, because of talk about them, she would have to leave. The Germans, with their fine sense of morality, did not approve of one of their officers sleeping with a Polish woman a third his age.

A few days later, when the major was away, Irene borrowed a horse and sleigh and she and her friends joined the others who were already hiding in the forest. One of her friends drove the sleigh dressed in one of Major Rugemer's uniforms. Seeing German soldiers saluting a Jew in a German uniform gave Irene an excuse to laugh.

One morning in March, as Irene was having coffee with Sigmund, the Polish forester, and his wife, Major Rugamer appeared outside Sigmund's cottage. Somehow he had found out where she was, and he had come to tell her the Russians were near, and she must not be captured by them. Therefore he would take her to Kielce, where he was to rejoin his regiment.

Later, parting from the major in Kielce, Irene realized that life is not all black and white. Rugamer was a German officer and had taken advantage of her, but he also cared for her and had saved her life and others, at the risk of his own. She realized that she had forgiven him.

In the spring of 1944 Irene was on her own again. Sigmund, the forester, had given her the names of Polish partisans in Kielce. She sought out a family named Ridel, who gladly took her in. Soon she met their son Janek, a leader of young Poles who were determined to resist both the Germans and the Russians and fight for their country's freedom.

Janek and Irene fell in love and agreed to marry on her birthday, May 5. But three days before the wedding Janek was killed during an ambush on a German convoy.

Irene helped bury her lover, then survived by throwing herself into the Polish underground, serving as a messenger who carried papers and news from one group to another. Early in 1945 she told the Ridels she must leave and try to find her own family, wherever they might be.

Irene learned that her father was dead. She could not find her mother and sisters. Lazar and Ida Hallar—who now had a son, Roman—took her in when she learned that the Russians were seeking her as a Polish partisan. In 1946 her friends convinced her that her best hope was to leave Poland. They helped her reach a relocation center in Germany. She arrived at the camp, in Bavaria, in June 1946, the only Catholic among hundreds of Jews. Such was the chaos of postwar Europe that three years passed before Irene was accepted for resettlement in the United States.

In the autumn of 1949, before she left for America, a delegation from the United Nations visited her camp, and one of the UN delegates asked to talk to her. He was a handsome man named William Opdyke and she told him her story through an interpreter. When she finished, he said, "It's an honor to know you, young lady. You're a person of uncommon courage. I hope you will be very happy in America. I know *we* will be proud to have you as a citizen."

When Irene arrived in New York City, she had no money, no job skills, no friends, and spoke no English. A refugee organization sent her to the garment district, where she was hired to operate a machine that made women's clothing. After two years she found a better job with a dressmaker. All the while she was learning English, and after five years she became a U.S. citizen.

One thing this lovely young woman did not do was go out with men. Her wartime experiences had left her terrified of them. She wore drab clothing and no makeup, so men would leave her alone. Her solitary life continued until 1956, when one day she was having coffee in a small coffee shop near the United Nations building. A man approached and said, "I know you."

He was William Opdyke, whom she had met seven years earlier in the German relocation camp. A widower, he asked her to dinner. Six weeks later they were married. Soon they moved to Arizona, where their daughter was

born, and later to Yorba Linda, California, where Bill Opdyke worked for the Chamber of Commerce.

"When my daughter was born, I put a Do Not Disturb
sign on my memory," Irene told me. "I didn't want to
think about the war or the Holocaust. I just wanted to
raise my little girl."

In the 1970s, Irene chanced to read a newspaper story
about the people who deny that the Holocaust took place.
Furious, she told her husband that she must speak out,
that such a monstrous lie could not go unchallenged. Her
husband, immensely proud of her wartime heroism, arranged for her to speak to the Yorba Linda Rotary Club.

She was trembling when she stood up to speak to the
Rotarians, but when she finished telling her story they
stood and cheered. It was the first of many speeches she
would make in Southern California and across America
and the world. Irene has made it her mission to tell the
truth about the Holocaust, especially to young people. She
has spoken at hundreds of schools, where the students in-
variably give her standing ovations and line up to express
their love and admiration.

Irene came to the attention of Rabbi Haim Asa of
Temple Beth Tikvah in Fullerton, California, who made
it his mission to have her heroism recognized by the Yad
Vashem, Israel's Holocaust authority. In time she was
awarded the Righteous Among the Nations Medal, one of
the highest honors Israel can bestow, and a tree was
planted on the Avenue of the Righteous in her honor. She
was included among the "Righteous Gentiles" who are
honored in the U.S. Holocaust Museum in Washington,
D.C. Eventually Irene was reunited with several of the Jews
she had saved—she even met Roman, the son of her friends
Ida and Lazar.

In 1984, after a report of one of her visits to Israel

appeared on Polish television, Irene received a letter from her sister Janina. She quickly flew to Poland where, miraculously, she was reunited with all four of her sisters.

When I visited Irene's home in Yorba Linda, she greeted me in her driveway, led me inside and introduced me to her visiting sister Wladja and two friends. Soon Irene and her sister were serving me a delicious Polish lunch of sausages, pierogies (Polish potato dumplings) and homemade breads. Irene, this dignified Polish woman, raised in a simple, God-fearing ethnic environment, reminded me so much of my own Croatian mother.

When I questioned her about her incredible courage and faith, her answers were simple.

She had acted instinctively, resisting evil because a love of humanity was embedded deep within her. Had she been afraid? Of course. "Many times I was frozen by fear for my own safety," she said. "But I couldn't turn my back on those innocent people. I knew that God was with me and had put me in the right place to serve. I had no time to think, 'You can do this' or 'You can't do this.' When I faced terrible decisions, always the right solution would somehow come to my mind."

She added, "Courage is a whisper from above. As long as you open your heart, you can hear the whisper. You mustn't listen with your mind, but with your heart."

She said she could risk her life, after her sister had left the factory, because she was only endangering herself. "The secret is, I was alone, without my sisters and parents, and if the Nazis caught me they would kill me, but not my parents or sisters. I was so angry at the Nazis. Why had they come to my country to kill people? I welcomed an opportunity to help. God put me in the right place to help."

Her beloved husband, Bill Opdyke, died four years

ago, and now Irene carries on alone. She is writing a book about her experiences, one aimed at young people. A group of her friends, along with business, religious and community leaders, have formed the Irene Gut Opdyke Holocaust Rescuer Foundation to raise money and teach young people to stand up against hate and bigotry. They plan to recognize outstanding young people with the Irene Opdyke Medal for Peace.

"I made it my vow that for the rest of my life I would speak out, particularly to young people," Irene said. "My job is to speak from the heart. I speak against hate, because hate is what causes war. I tell young people what happened to me, and I tell them, 'You are the future leaders. Reach out to each other. We are all the same. You are the last generation that will hear eyewitness testimony to what happened. Reach out. Hate doesn't accomplish anything. Think how lucky you are to live in a free country.' "

My visit with Irene ended with an unexpected epiphany.

We were sitting side by side in one corner of her living room. Bright sunlight streamed in the window and caught this beautiful woman in a golden haze. We had been talking about faith. She said she believes there are many ways to God.

But, she added, "Jesus is my Lord."

Irene took my hand and recited the entire Twenty-third Psalm. I have heard the psalm many times, but I had never appreciated its poetry, its music, its full meaning, until I heard it spoken by this woman who truly had walked through the valley of the shadow of death, who truly had feared no evil and who surely will dwell in the house of the Lord forever.

When we parted a few minutes later, I could not say if

she is a saint or simply an extraordinarily good and brave human being. But of this I am sure: a hundred years from now, when most of the celebrated names of our era are long forgotten, the world will still ponder the goodness and greatness of Irene Gut Opdyke.

One Pair of Shoes
at a Time

Albert Lexie

It was my friend Stu Boehmig, pastor of the Orchard Hill Church in Pittsburgh, who told me about Albert Lexie. "You must meet this man," he said. "He's remarkable." For the past forty years Albert, who has a mental disability, has supported himself by shining shoes. Since 1981 he has shined shoes two days a week at the Children's Hospital of Pittsburgh and given his tips to the hospital's Free Care Fund. His donations have totaled nearly $40,000, and he has made himself the soul of this great medical institution.

ONE THURSDAY in December, joined by my friend Ron Hartman, I accompanied Albert Lexie on his rounds at the Children's Hospital in Pittsburgh.

It wasn't easy to keep up with him. Albert is a man of great enthusiasm and great determination. He races around the hospital, carrying his thirty-five pound shoeshine box on a strap around his neck, taking stairs because they're faster than elevators, determined to see all of the doctors, nurses and administrators who are expecting him. The box is heavy and bulky, but he weaves through the crowded corridors like a broken field runner, determined to stay on schedule. People call, "Hi, Albert!" or "Hello, Mr. Celebrity" (he won a recent award for community service) but he barely notices. When one of his customers is too busy to see him immediately, Albert will probably leave and come back later. He has to keep moving. He has to shine the shoes to make the money to help his kids.

Albert is a solidly built man of fifty-five whose black hair is showing signs of gray. He wears thick glasses that he often pushes back up his nose. The day I met him, he was dressed in a white polo shirt, wrinkled gray pants, a Children's Hospital apron and black wingtip shoes that were literally falling apart—he is too busy caring for other people's shoes to worry about his own.

His first customer that day, Dr. Michael Painter, a pediatric neurologist, told us, as Albert began a vigorous, expert, six-minute shoeshine, "I've been Albert's customer for five years. It's a great shoeshine and it benefits the hospital."

Over his shoulder, Albert asks the doctor's assistant, Denise Antonelli, to call his next customer and say he is running late. "I'm Albert's part-time secretary," she joked. "I've known him for fifteen years. At first he came to the hospital once a week but he got so busy he started coming twice."

Once Dr. Painter's shoes were glistening, Albert raced to the hospital's human resources office, where three customers waited. The first, Bob Nolan, a human resources representative, told me: "Albert is dedicated. He does it for the kids, not for himself. It's inspirational." The next customer, Todd Purvis, the hospital's director of human resources, told me: "Albert and I go back five years, to my first week here." Tom Majewski, the hospital's employee-relations manager, said: "Albert is dedicated to this institution. We've all grown to respect him. You always find time for Albert, even on the busiest days. He's the spirit of the hospital."

Last year Majewski helped Albert celebrate his fifteenth anniversary at the hospital. He also tried to help him drum up new business by sending out e-mail messages reminding employees of Albert's services and advertising the special anniversary rate Albert was offering ($1.75 instead of $2.00), along with gifts like coffee cups.

Albert had pasted a notice to the side of his shoeshine box saying "Albert's Kids Total As Of 12-16-97—$1317.40." At Albert's request, the hospital's development office keeps a record of his donations on a February-to-February basis, because he started at the hospital in February 1981. Thus, that amount was his donation to the Free Care Fund for the first ten months of this year. Albert keeps the $2.00 he charges for a shine and donates his tips, and other donations that come in, to the Fund. Most people add a dollar tip, but some hand over a $5.00 bill and tell him to keep the change. He's headed for around $1500 this year, not a good year for Albert. In 1996 he donated $3174, which included his $1000 prize for winning a Jefferson Award for community service. The two previous years he donated $1727 and $2062. One year he gave $4500, in part because of a lawyer who raffled off a television set and gave Albert the proceeds.

In addition to Tuesdays and Thursdays at the Children's Hospital, Albert shines shoes three days a week in the towns of Charleroi, Monessen, Donora and Monongahela; those tips also go to the hospital fund. Albert estimates that he has about a hundred regular customers each week. Sometime in 1998, his total donations to the Children's Hospital since 1981 will pass $40,000. "He's done that one pair of shoes at a time," says Dr. Jonathan Finder, one of Albert's "best buddies" at the hospital. Albert's Fund, as it is known, is part of the hospital's Free Care Fund, which in 1997 paid for $9.1 million worth of care for children whose families live within a hundred miles of the hospital. Albert dreams of doing even more. "I'm going to build up my business and give ten times as much!" he declares proudly.

The Children's Hospital of Pittsburgh is recognized worldwide for its organ transplant program, and another of Albert's customers that morning was Dr. Samuel Kocoshis, who is part of a team that has done pioneering work in bowel transplants. As Albert worked on his shoes, the good-natured doctor said, only partly in jest, "Albert is probably the best businessman in this institution. He's also the most reliable. It's really the best of business. His customers profit by it. The hospital profits by it. The children profit by it.

Albert told us that one of his greatest thrills comes when hospital officials arrange for him to tour one of the wards and meet with some of the children his donations have helped. "I see the kids once a month," he said. "I give 'em a gift or a baseball card. They're my sweeties."

"On his birthday, the kids made Albert a card," Dr. Kocoshis added. "You'd have thought he won the lottery. He showed it to everyone."

After shining ten pairs of shoes, Albert agreed to let me and Ron take him to a late lunch at Hemingway's, a popular restaurant near the hospital that one of the doctors recommended. Albert had never been there before—he usually eats in the hospital cafeteria—but he was no stranger. As we entered, a young woman from the hospital greeted him in the doorway. After we settled in our booth, another young woman from the hospital came over from a nearby table to show Albert her newborn daughter. Clearly, Albert was a celebrity.

Over lunch, Albert told us more about his life. He was born and raised in nearby Monessen, where my father grew up. Albert and his brother and sister were raised by their mother. In a high school shop class, when Albert was fifteen, he built a shoeshine box, and soon he left to make his living by shining shoes. At first he worked in bars but he didn't like that so he began to work in stores. For a time, he had a little shop in Monessen, which in 1977 celebrated Albert Lexie Day to honor him for twenty years of service to the community.

Albert continued to seek out other towns and locations. In 1981 he began to shine shoes one day a week at the Children's Hospital. In those days a well-known father-and-daughter television team in Pittsburgh, Bill and

Patti Burns, put on an annual telethon to benefit the hospital. Albert was a great fan of Patti Burns and, after a friend took him to the telethon, he decided to donate the $750 savings in his bank account to the telethon. After that he started donating all his tips to the hospital.

Albert lives alone in a high-rise apartment building in Monessen. To reach the hospital before eight on Tuesdays and Thursdays, he catches a bus before six in the morning; he repeats the two-hour, $3.40 round trip in the evening. One of his friends at the hospital says, "I think Albert is a little scared on that bus ride—he prays for safe passage." On weekends, Albert says he "loafs," except for Sunday morning services at the Riverside Tabernacle, a Pentecostal church, where he sings in the choir. He also watches television, mostly the religious channel, and his apartment is filled with tapes of the gospel music that he loves.

After lunch we hurried back to the hospital so Albert could meet his goal of shining twenty pairs of shoes that day. We raced down several flights of stairs to the hospital's facilities offices in the basement where more customers awaited him. Many people told us they get a shine from Albert each week, whether they need one or not. The Children's Hospital of Pittsburgh may well have the best-shined shoes of any hospital in the world.

Albert has a unique and wonderful personality. He is totally honest, very pleasant and utterly caring. When you talk, he gives you his total, undivided attention. He is not quick to judge. He is an oasis amid the intense pressures of the hospital, and an inspiration. Albert's sweetness and sincerity make him a very special part of the world he lives in. Often we move too fast and miss too much in our lives. Albert reminds us to slow down, look beneath the veneer and marvel at life.

Around two-thirty Albert led us to the third-floor

office of Dr. Jonathan Finder, a pediatric pulmonary specialist, and an assistant professor of pediatrics at the University of Pittsburgh. Dr. Finder is an outgoing man of thirty-seven whose passions include the banjo. He has been a regular of Albert's for more than four years. Last year a nurse, Connie Richless, told him about the Jefferson Awards, which are presented annually on both the local and national levels, and are intended to honor ordinary people who do extraordinary things.

In 1997 more than 20,000 people were nominated for these awards. The local sponsors include newspapers and television stations, and as a result the winners often receive much-deserved recognition. Dr. Finder thought Albert was just the sort of unsung hero the Jefferson Awards were meant to honor, so he sent in a nomination for him.

Albert was thrilled. "He kept saying, 'I'm going to win an award,'" Dr. Finder recalls. As it turned out, Albert was right. He was one of the seven men and women chosen for an Outstanding Citizen award by the local sponsors. Albert and the other winners were asked to speak at the awards dinner early in 1997. "I want to thank all of you and thank the Lord," he told the audience. "Without Him, this wouldn't have happened. The Lord gets all the credit for what I do."

As a result of the award, the *Pittsburgh Post-Gazette* carried an excellent article on Albert that was later condensed by the *Reader's Digest*. With all the publicity, Albert's friends at the hospital teased him a little about being a celebrity. Albert doesn't mind—he wishes he'd been chosen to represent Pittsburgh at the national awards ceremony in Washington, D.C., where he had hoped to tour the White House.

As Dr. Finder finished telling us about the Jefferson Award, Albert was busy shining his shoes. He and Albert share a love of music—the doctor is a fervent bluegrass fan who keeps a photograph of Bill Monroe, the father of bluegrass, on the wall of his small office. He mentioned that the previous summer Albert had ridden a Greyhound bus to a nearby town to attend a gospel concert and had stayed overnight in a Days Inn.

"I had a great time," Albert declared. "I'm going back again." Unexpectedly, he added, "Do you mind if I sing you a song?"

We replied that we would be honored. Albert was still kneeling as he began to sing "The Old Rugged Cross." By the time he reached the great final lines about exchanging his cross for a crown, doctors and nurses had gathered outside the door to listen and applaud.

The experts say that Albert does not have the intellectual capacity that most of us have. That may be true. But I know this: if in heaven we can indeed exchange our crosses for a crown, no crown in paradise will shine more brightly than Albert Lexie's.

A Sacred
Space

Nancy Carver

How do we die? Alone, afraid and in pain? Or content, cared for and surrounded by our loved ones? Increasingly, Americans are dying a good death, often helped by the fast-growing hospice movement. In recent years thousands of hospice programs have begun, all over America. One of the best is located in Oklahoma City, a city that has known much pain and much courage. Meeting its staff and volunteers, my thoughts went back to a time when I urgently needed help in dealing with my own grief.

MY PARENTS, John and Anne Kasich, were the children of immigrants, from Czechoslovakia on my dad's side and from Yugoslavia on my mother's. My dad served in the army during World War II. He met my mother after the war when they were both working for the Veterans Administration. My dad went to work for the post office and delivered mail for twenty-nine years. His route included our own home in McKees Rocks, Pennsylvania. Once my brother and sister and I were enrolled in school, my mother worked nights at the Pittsburgh post office. My parents were hardworking, frugal people. They didn't drink or smoke. My mother would walk a mile to avoid spending a quarter on a bus. It was a thrill for them to go out and splurge on coffee and a doughnut. They went to church every Sunday and sent three kids to college with no help from anyone.

My parents were sixty-seven years old, in perfect health, and enjoying their retirement when a drunk driver crashed into their car as they were leaving a Burger King one August evening in 1987. A doctor called me at midnight to tell me my father was dead and my mother was in critical condition. I drove all night from Washington and reached the hospital at dawn. When I arrived, the doctors were operating on my mother so I lay down on a sofa in a waiting room. I was in shock. It was like entering a black hole.

After a while a man named Bill Dinello, the hospital's trauma social worker, offered to help me in any way he could. I don't remember much of what we talked about. Bill told me later that I asked a lot of questions about the accident and my mother's condition. He told me that was normal. People often try to gather information instead of confronting their grief. Bill let me lie down in his office where I could be alone with my sorrow.

Later that morning, after my mother died, Stu Boehmig, the assistant pastor at her Episcopal church, tried to comfort me. When he said he knew how I felt, I replied heatedly that he didn't know how I felt, that no one could know how I felt.

"You're right," Stu agreed. "But I do know that your mother would rather be with her Lord than anywhere else."

Stu went on to say something that was vitally important to me: "You've got to decide if you want to have a relationship with God. You have a window of opportunity that is open now but in time will pass."

I knew he was right. I'd gotten away from religion. Now I knew I had nowhere else to go. I don't know how people survive that kind of pain without faith. My parents' death started a transformation of my life, a journey to discover God and to rediscover myself. Religion became a source of strength and solace. With faith, I learned, comes peace.

Bill Dinello, Stu Boehmig and many others helped me when I urgently needed help, asking only that I do the same for others in return. Since then I've tried to help people in need, and I've come to have great respect for those whose life's work is to comfort others. I began to look around me and see how many people are doing good work, God's work, in so many ways. Several friends told me about the hospice movement, and the comfort it brings to dying people and their families. When I started this book, I asked Naomi Naierman, president of the American Hospice Foundation, if she could recommend an outstanding program. She said that Nancy Carver, at Hospice Care of Oklahoma, directed one of the most innovative bereavement programs in America. As a result, I traveled to Oklahoma City, where I met some of the most loving, caring, courageous people I've ever known.

The word "hospice" comes from a medieval word for a place of shelter for travelers on difficult journeys. The modern hospice movement began in England in the 1960s with the work of Dr. Cicely Saunders, and in the United States in the 1970s with the work of Dr. Elizabeth Kübler-Ross. At first the movement was limited to volunteers who helped their friends and neighbors die in comfort at home, in their own beds, rather than in a hospital.

Modern medicine is extremely good at keeping people alive, but when an illness is terminal, many doctors don't know what to do, although the patient's spiritual and emotional needs may be greater than ever. During the 1970s it became clear that hospice care was not only compassionate, but it offered a less expensive way for people to die than hospitalization. Both factors led Congress to pass legislation in 1983 that authorized Medicare to pay for hospice care. For a patient to qualify, his or her primary care doctor must certify that he or she has less than six months to live. Patients, of course, must want the hospice treatment and must be willing to give up "curative" or life-prolonging treatment in favor of "palliative" care that focuses on keeping them comfortable.

Once Medicare funds became available, hospice programs began to spread rapidly. Most are nonprofit, but some are for-profit operations. In either case, they are paid an average of about $95 a day per patient for home care. One study said that for every dollar spent on hospice Medicare saved $1.52. Hospice care is given, of course, in the final stages of illness when hospital care becomes extremely expensive. There are some residential hospice programs, but most focus on helping patients in their homes. The programs make available a team of doctors, nurses, social workers and volunteers who go to the home as needed to care for the patient and to teach the patient's family how to provide care. Already, half the people who die of cancer in America have had hospice care, yet overall only two in ten who die use the program. By 1997 there were more than 3000 hospices in America, and more than 70 in Oklahoma, where Nancy Carver works.

Nancy is a tall, slender woman with long, curly brown hair and a gentle manner. She grew up on a farm in Nebraska. Her grandparents came from Germany and brought with them a distrust of government, and of authority in general, that Nancy inherited. She won a scholarship to Grinnell College and in 1974 became the first of her family to graduate from college. She married a lawyer and had two daughters, but the marriage ended in divorce and in 1980 she went to work as a social worker in Cedar Rapids, Iowa. By 1991 she had risen to be the director of a mental health program in Norman, Oklahoma, but she wasn't receiving the satisfaction she wanted from her work.

Her life had begun to change in 1989 when, as the result of an accident, she was clinically dead for three and a half minutes: "I felt myself traveling at a great rate of speed, yet not moving. I was in total darkness. I knew I was dead and I was quite comfortable with it. I was totally at peace. I was coming home. I saw a light and was part of the light. All my life I'd thought it was important to be right and now I felt I'd received a message telling me that being right was not what life was about. Then I was sent back—I couldn't resist. When I woke up in the emergency room, I told the doctor, 'I'm supposed to be dead—I want to go back.' Later I met others who'd had near-death experiences, who had drowned or died on the operating table. We all had the same feelings. No fear of death, a longing to go back home, and a need to do something important with our lives."

Nancy calls herself a seeker. Her goal is a spiritual, God-directed life. She became a Quaker a few years ago, and she meditates twice a day, seeking clarity. After her near-death experience, she was all the more determined that her work should offer her a spiritual dimension.

"I asked, 'What is the gift I have to offer? How am I meant to serve?'" She had been impressed by what she'd heard about the hospice movement. ("I thought, 'This is not like other government programs—this is too good to be true.'") In 1994, when someone told her that the Family Hospice in Oklahoma City was looking for a social worker, she called immediately and was hired.

Nancy still recalls her first hospice patient: "She was eighty-nine years old, so I thought, 'Good, I got an easy one!' But it turned out that she was very angry about dying. I said, 'When did you expect to die?' She said, 'When I was ready!'"

Nancy had been working for a year at the Family Hospice when, in the aftermath of the April 19, 1995, bombing of the Alfred Murrah Federal Building, she received a call from Hospice Care of Oklahoma, which needed a bereavement coordinator. At first she was uncertain about the move because Hospice Care of Oklahoma is a for-profit program. "I had a snooty idea that for-profit was morally wrong—but I was wrong. Our program is for-profit and I

A Sacred Space

think it's the best hospice in the county. They let me run the kind of program I want, and no one is turned away for lack of money or insurance."

The move was significant for Nancy because it meant shifting her professional focus from the dying to their survivors. "I thought I had the right skills to do grief work," she says. "I wanted to focus on loss. Most people prefer to work with the dying, but after the bombing, I had a clear leading to do bereavement work. It was a dramatic change for me."

Hospice Care of Oklahoma's staff includes more than thirty professionals, including a medical director, nurses, social workers, therapists, health care aides and a spiritual care coordinator, plus about fifty volunteers. The program usually serves about sixty patients and their families at a time. Six registered nurses serve as case managers and direct a team of staff and volunteers who work with patients as they are needed. One of their goals is to get family members involved in preparing food, giving medicine and baths, and otherwise caring for the patient.

The hospice movement believes that no one should die in needless pain. Pain management, through medication, is the medical side of hospice. Many family doctors are not well informed about painkillers and are reluctant to prescribe them. Hospice doctors can advise them on dosages that will relieve pain while still leaving the patient alert.

Hospice services are essentially simple, but Nancy believes they address difficult problems in our society. "In our culture, you're supposed to be young and healthy and problem-free. Dying people are put outside our cultural circle. It's a challenge to do hospice work in a death-avoiding society. So many people are in denial."

Hospice starts with the official recognition that the patient is likely to die within six months. Often, doctors don't want to make that admission, because they see it as a failure on their part. Moreover, patients and families can also be reluctant to admit that death is near. As a result, hospice services are often put off until death is very near. Nationally, the average period of care is not six months but less than two months. Those in the movement think it is tragic when dying people don't take advantage of hospice. Often it is simply because they and their doctors don't know about the program. As a result, the hospice staff conducts an active outreach campaign to make doctors and the community aware of their services.

The goal of hospice, simply put, is to help people achieve "a good death," but that means more than simply providing comfort and reducing pain. It may also involve reconciliation with loved ones. Asked to describe a good death, Nancy and her colleagues often tell of bringing together a patient and an estranged child or other family member; only then could the patient die at peace.

Often, Nancy says, family members avoid the death of a loved one, but the sooner they become involved the less guilt and sorrow they will feel later. She points out that, amid the national debate over assisted suicide, hospice offers a better path: if dying people are given adequate medication and loving care, they are much less likely to choose suicide.

Hospice Care of Oklahoma's offices are located on the eleventh floor of a medical building a mile or so from downtown Oklahoma City. One afternoon I sat in its conference room with Nancy and two of her colleagues, Jean Calder, the program's administrator, and Polly Keenan, a registered nurse. I asked each what had drawn her to hospice and what it meant to her.

Nancy had already spoken of her search for spirituality and her near-death experience, but now she told us that when she was six years old she had measles and gave them to her pregnant mother, which caused her brother to die at birth and almost killed her mother. She heard the grown-ups whispering that she had killed her brother, and she carried that guilt for many years. If she had been given the counseling and support that she now gives others, she could have been spared decades of guilt and pain.

"People who work here feel led here," Nancy said. "They're meant to be here. They've found their gift. At night, sometimes I go home and think I've gotten so much more out of this than my patients. I think we work in a sacred space with people as they leave this world. You're a channel for grace, a messenger. The dying create the sacred space by the things they say and do. If you want to live a spiritual life, there's no better place than where people are dying. Death is a blessing, the same as birth. It's coming full circle."

Jean Calder, Hospice Care of Oklahoma's administrator, directs all aspects of the program. A nurse for many years, she says, "I'll be returning to the field—that's where my heart is.

"I don't often speak of this," she told us, "but I had a son die within twenty-four hours of birth. My husband was wonderful, but aside from him I wasn't comforted. I didn't have the grief support I needed. People didn't understand the need back then. Later, I had a neck injury, and didn't have the help I needed with the pain. Both these experiences drew me to hospice, which works with both physical and spiritual pain. It's the concept of the 'wounded healer.' I wanted things to be different for others."

Jean recalled one of her earliest patients. "His name was Joseph. He lived alone and when I first arrived he was drinking and belligerent. I wasn't sure I could help him. But his face lit up after our team arrived and he never drank again. We gave a sixty-ninth birthday party for him and tears rolled down his face. He said he'd never had a birthday party before. His life was turned around in six months. He went to his sister's home for his last few days and he died with a smile on his face. Our team still meets to celebrate his birthday."

Polly Keenan, the third person I met with, is a strong-minded, fun-loving woman who in 1991 was a successful Oklahoma City real estate agent. One day, approaching a traffic light, she decided that if the light stayed red she would go directly to her business meeting, but if it turned green she would stop and get her car washed. The light turned green. The people who washed her car changed the station on her radio, and when Polly drove on she found herself listening to a talk show that she wouldn't normally have heard.

The person being interviewed was a doctor who was just back from Romania, where he had worked with children who had been "warehoused" by the corrupt communist government of Nicolae Ceauşescu. The government had stolen babies from their families to sell on the international black market, and those that were judged unsuitable for adoption were put in hospitals in inhumane conditions. Polly, moved by the doctor's account, told herself, "If I had medical experience, I'd go there and help." Just then, the doctor said, "We take one nonmedical person on each team." That cinched the deal, and soon Polly was in Romania working with children who, she says angrily, "had been treated like caged animals."

"When I returned to this country, I was fifty-five years old and finally knew what I wanted to do with my life,"

Polly says. "When people ask how I decided to be a nurse, I tell them, 'Because of a green light.' Of course, I think it was an act of God."

Early in her nursing career, Polly found the special talent that drew her to hospice work. "I have a gift for being with dying people. Other nurses would ask me to stay with their terminal patients. I have a real comfortable feeling with people who are dying. I see myself as a bridge to wherever they are going. Not many people can walk in and deal with it. The more I give my patients, the more I receive. It's an awesome thing to be with someone at their death. I don't think you can be any more intimate than that. I pray every day that people will see my spirituality and it will help them touch their own."

Nancy, Jean and Polly each told me their lives were changed by the 1995 bombing of the federal building in Oklahoma City. When each learned of the disaster, she rushed to the scene or to a nearby hospital to help. They did not often counsel survivors of bombing victims; that was handled by a federally financed program called Operation Heartland. But they feel that the tragedy changed Oklahoma City and made their work more important than ever. Each knew people who were killed or injured. They tell poignant stories of the bombing's aftermath: The mother of a bombing victim who, after the explosion of TWA Flight 800, wrote the family of each of its victims to share what she had learned of loss and suffering; the father of a young woman killed in the blast who often returns to the site to talk to strangers about his daughter and her life. Polly told me, "I think that people in Oklahoma City joined together and pooled their strength and passed it on to those who needed it."

Nancy says the families of some victims are upset because they feel that their loved ones are being remembered more for how they died rather than how they lived. In the long run, she says, how a person lived is always more important. It has troubled her when survivors have looked to the trials of the alleged bombers to ease their pain. "People think justice will heal them, but they may find it's hollow. The grief goes on. We learned a lot from the bombing about the power of grief."

Volunteers are central to any hospice program. The 1983 legislation decreed that, to qualify for Medicare payments, at least five percent of a program's hours of service must be provided by volunteers. Naea Teachman, the volunteer coordinator, says that for her program it is more like fifteen or twenty percent. Often the volunteers are people whom hospice helped when their own loved ones were dying. "After a death, people search for meaning," Nancy Carver says. "Part of the meaning of death may be helping others."

Hospice doesn't stop when a patient dies. The program also helps survivors deal with their grief. Nancy Carver thinks our society pays far too little attention to the survivors. "In the first three months, I just ask people to survive. That's what it takes human beings to get over this kind of loss. They're asking, 'Can I hurt this bad and live?' Yet the standard bereavement leave for workers is three days."

Nancy wants to change the way society treats people who are grieving. "We need more social support for people. It's not that they can't work or go to school, but they need help. At work, we need to educate supervisors on what people are going through. They may cry sometimes. They may have trouble making decisions. They may need a safe haven, away from their work station, where they can go and regroup. They may need someone to talk to.

They may need additional leave time they can make up later. It's the same for students at school. They don't need to drop out and lose a year but they need support. It's not expensive. It's just education and support."

After a patient dies, hospice sends surviving family members letters offering assistance. Some people want no assistance, but others may want someone to come by for regular visits. Support groups help people recover and make new friends. Nancy has pioneered the use of poetry, music and movies to help people deal with grief. "There are good books on grief," she says, "but often people just can't focus on reading. We show movies that deal with death, like *In the Gloaming, Shadowlands* and *I Never Sang for My Father.* They start people talking and thinking."

Nancy encourages survivors to express their feelings in poetry, and she has published a volume of poems, called *Love After Death,* that were written by bereaved people. The first and last poems in the volume were written by Mamie Yandle, who in 1996 lost her husband of forty-two years, Bobby Gene Yandle.

I met Mamie, a silver-haired woman in her sixties whose courage, proud bearing and self-reliance called to mind the pioneer women who settled the American West.

"In April 1996 they removed Bob's kidney and found a cancer that was spreading fast," Mamie told me. "He had the option of chemotherapy, but he didn't want it. He'd had a good life. We'd been very happy, and had two children and a grandchild. He said he'd rather have thirty days of a good life than a year of suffering like so many we'd seen. He asked me if it would bother me for him to die at home. I told him it would be an honor for him to die in our home.

"I'd been a nurse for many years, and seen many people die, but nothing prepares you for what it's like to lose your mate. You really are part of each other. I told him, 'I won't be crying, but my heart will be breaking.' I didn't want to upset him, so I'd go into the bathroom or out into the woods to do my crying."

Over the summer Mamie cared for her husband as he gradually grew weaker. On October 6 they celebrated their forty-second wedding anniversary. On the first Tuesday in November they went to vote, but the next day, when Bob felt too bad to meet his best friend for coffee, Mamie knew he was getting worse. By Friday night she knew the end was near.

"I knew in my heart he would die that night. I got him in bed and slipped off my shoes and got in beside him and loved him up. I decided I wouldn't sleep that night. I was going to talk to him. I went back through the years and brought back memories. I told him I love him. He was patting my hand. At two in the morning, I noticed a change in his breathing. He had made me promise I wouldn't let our children watch him die. I felt torn but I'd made the promise. He began to sweat. I took his blood pressure and it was going down. I didn't call our minister or our friends. He wanted this to be a private thing. I did wake our son at three and ask him to call his sister. Bob finally went into a coma. He was breathing deep, gasping breaths. At dawn I opened the blinds and let the sun in. It was a beautiful day. I gave him a light bath and put clean pajamas on him. Our son came in and was telling him he loved him. I knew Bob could hear. We just kept loving on him and patting him, and finally, at about seven-thirty, I said, 'Honey, just let go. God is waiting. The children love you. You've been a good husband and father. Don't worry about me. Just let go.' At eight-fifteen he drew his last breath. My arms were around him and his son was holding on to him. I think sometimes they need permission to go."

Mamie had not called upon hospice until that final weekend, because of her determination to care for her husband herself, but the program became important to her later.

"Nancy asked if she could visit me sometimes. I wanted to handle it myself, because I'm a private person, but I loved that lady from the moment I saw her. She sits and listens and lets you pour out your heart. She is so wise. No one has helped me like Nancy. She's a very dear friend."

I asked Nancy what it was that she offered to people like Mamie. "The greatest gift I can give them is no expectations," she replied. "It's hard, because I have a lot of ideas about grief, but I have to put my ideas aside and walk with them wherever their grief takes them. Sometimes I'm frightened by the magnitude of the grief I see, by how overwhelming and desolate it is. It almost seems hopeless. But I'm a merchant of hope. I have to bring hope and love. I have to challenge the view of a world without hope. There is an innate wisdom in the human organism. If we're given encouragement, we heal. We move toward light and healing. We must never give up on anyone. We grow. My message to people is: Don't waste time being afraid, not of cancer, not of death. There is a terrible and beautiful power in the world. It unfolds, and the circle truly is unbroken."

I left Oklahoma City with so many enduring memories of the courageous people I met there. I remember Rebecca Pipkin, one member of the hospice staff, saying, "One day I saw both a birth and a death. I saw one soul enter this world and another one leave it. What could be more wonderful than that?" By confronting the reality of death, by honoring those who must die, thousands of hospice workers, and other grief counselors, all across America, enrich all our lives. Their work reminds us that none of us is immune to tragedy, and all of us must help one another, when sooner or later it arrives.

CONCLUSION

Writing this book has been a great adventure. It has taken me places I had not been before and introduced me to scores of wonderful people I would not otherwise have known. To find people such as the heroes in this book was not hard. There are plenty of them out there, doing good works every day—not for money or publicity, but because they believe that what they're doing is right. If I'd had time, I could have found hundreds more for every one I describe here—and I hope I can someday.

A friend gave me a list of twelve volunteer programs in Los Angeles that led me to Schools on Wheels. In Detroit, Barbara Gattorn, who works with the Greater Detroit Chamber of Commerce, wrote to me recommending three programs. They were Focus: HOPE, which works on behalf of inner-city youth; it was started by Father Bill Cunningham and, after his death, carried on by Eleanor Josaitis; the Rev. Eddie Edwards's Joy of Jesus program, which also works in the inner city; and Loretta Nagle's Angels' House. "To be in the presence of each of these three people is an ethereal experience," Barbara wrote. "They are the personification of humility, in spite of their great deeds. I have spent personal and professional time with each of them and always leave feeling very insignificant." I chose to write about Loretta Nagle because I wanted to discuss the developmentally disabled, but I have no doubt that I would have been just as impressed and moved by the other two programs. Given more time, I would also have written about the Mobile Meals Service in Spartanburg, South Carolina, which has recruited hundreds of volunteers to serve more than a thousand meals a day, five days a week. There are so many fine people and fine programs, coast to coast.

We need to recognize what a priceless national resource pioneers such as these are, and never underestimate their impact. Some, like Jack McConnell and Gretchen Buchenholz, have started ambitious, big-budget programs. Others work anonymously, volunteering to make sandwiches with Amber Coffman or reading to terminally ill people in hospice programs. We need to honor them all, just as we now honor the athletes and entertainers who achieve vast fame and fortune. Bill Cosby and Cal Ripkin are great human beings and role models, but so are Jack McConnell, Geoff Canada and Agnes Stevens. We need to expand our concept of greatness to honor them as well.

Sometimes I think we see the trees but not the forest. The media report on individual volunteers, but I think we do not fully appreciate that they are part of a rapidly growing national crusade, and its sum is even greater than its parts. In recent years many concerned citizens have recognized that government can't solve all our problems. It is up to individuals to take up the challenge. This movement doesn't have a name—I call it the new volunteerism—but it contains tens of millions of Americans and it is spreading and changing our society.

One of the most encouraging and exciting things about the new volunteerism is that today's volunteer is often tomorrow's activist. People who care about improving society may decide to take the next step, whether it is attending school board meetings, joining in a political campaign or even running for office. And that's good. Too often power over our lives drifts to politicians and bureaucrats by default. If you care enough to volunteer, you may decide to stand up and be heard in other ways.

Most of the people I have written about are motivated by religious faith. It wasn't that religion played a role in choosing them: I was just looking for interesting, worthwhile programs. But time after time the people I met told me it was faith that kept them going. At a time when many people debate the role of religion in our political system, it's worthwhile to note the important work this faith-based movement is quietly accomplishing. All of us, whatever our views, are needed and welcome in addressing our social needs, but my travels convinced me that today's explosion of volunteerism is largely a spiritual outpouring.

There is increasing recognition of the vital role that churches play in helping people in need, particularly in poor neighborhoods. With this realization has come a growing demand for government to fund faith-based social programs. Often, they are the strongest institutions in inner-city neighborhoods. To many of today's young ministers, community service is what the civil rights movement was to an earlier generation. I believe that the call for funding of faith-based community programs does not violate the separation of church and state, although we do need clarifying laws and court decisions that will enable us to take full advantage of these programs.

When I interviewed people, I often asked what had made them so willing to make personal sacrifices to help others. Almost always, in one way or another, they said, "My parents" or "It was how I was raised." They were shaped by their families; to know them is to be reminded that the family is the incubator of all that is best in us. Families teach us values, responsibility and faith. We can't go back and change our families or how we were raised. But we can make sure that, as we raise our own children, we give them the kind of solid, loving, caring foundation they need to become adults who care about more than their own well-being. John Donne wrote many years ago that no man is an island, for we are all part of the great mainland of humanity. The people profiled in this book understand that enduring truth, and we must understand it too.

Time after time, we see that people *want* to help if they are shown a way. When Jack McConnell, Amber Coffman, Karen Olson and Agnes Stevens created vehicles for service, volunteers flocked to them. It's the "field of dreams" approach—build it and they will come. There are millions of Americans volunteering now, and that is wonderful, but their ranks can and should be doubled. That is the great challenge we face.

The role of government should be focused. It should not be an obstacle to human achievement. I described the ways government has hampered the growth of Cheryl Krueger's cookie company. Like any member of Congress, I could tell you a hundred stories I've heard from people who've been frustrated by government interference. Here's one. A Texas businessman, who had risen from poverty to success, took pride in regarding his employees as part of a family. Employees were welcome to bring their children to the plant, and when they did, he would give the kids a safe, simple chore to perform, then pay them the minimum wage for the time they worked. It was a way to let young people earn a little money and have a feeling of accomplishment.

When one employee brought her eleven-year-old to

the office, the businessman let the boy spend a few hours sealing boxes, and at the end of the day he wrote the boy a check. The businessman forgot all about it—until the U.S. Department of Labor called. The woman had left the company and for some reason she told the Labor Department about her son's few hours of work. Labor Department officials told the businessman he was being fined a thousand dollars for violating the child labor laws. "I didn't mind the money," he said. "But I had to stop doing something I thought was helping young people. I had to become someone who wasn't me."

Congress, the courts, the White House and individuals must oppose this kind of blind overregulation. It doesn't just demoralize one businessman—it saps our national spirit. Restoring the vitality of America means reducing government excesses and restoring our capacity for self-government. When government becomes too powerful it is because we the people have let it, by being passive, by being indifferent, by creating a power vacuum that government has eagerly filled.

We must break the government "trusts" just as Teddy Roosevelt broke the trusts of business.

Regulators should be required to use cost-analysis calculations and common sense in their dealings with citizens. Sunsetting legislation should be used to guarantee that federal programs and regulations must justify their existence. We cannot tolerate government regulations—local, state or federal—that cripple the ability of individuals or organizations to serve the community.

Local people can best solve local problems. When the federal government assists local programs, it should be a limited partner, providing funding without strings and government-imposed models.

We should receive tax credits when we give money to

community social programs. In other words, our money would go directly to the local programs, rather than to the U.S. Treasury. We would still have programs to help people, but we would shift the balance toward those that are locally designed and operated.

In Congress, I've fought a long battle against what I call corporate welfare. By that, I mean special tax breaks or other favoritism for powerful corporations that aren't given to the average citizen. For example, I've opposed funds to corporations to advertise their products overseas or to start operations overseas. Still, even as a foe of corporate abuses, I'm glad to praise the corporations that have done an outstanding job of philanthropic giving. According to the *Taft Corporate Giving Directory*, the ten top corporate givers in 1996 were: Merck & Company, IBM, Johnson & Johnson, Pfizer Inc., Hewlett-Packard, General Motors, Eli Lilly & Company, Bristol-Myers Squibb Company, Microsoft, Intel Corporation. The first corporation on the list donated more than $140 million; the tenth more than $55 million. Often corporations employ talented people who work hard to seek out and fund effective local programs. Let's applaud them for the money they give and the good they do, and encourage others to do the same.

We in Congress must do more to support the new volunteerism. We must rise above party and get behind programs that work. We must find bipartisan solutions and not worry about who gets the credit. There's too much petty partisan bickering in Washington today. Debate is healthy, but so is finding areas of agreement. Sometimes in politics both sides can win.

I'm part of a Bible study group that meets regularly in Washington. I often joke (except it's not really a joke) that it's the only meeting I attend that no one wants to see end. As we sit there, Democrats and Republicans alike, having serious, vigorous, joyous discussions of spiritual issues, sometimes I have a fantasy that the entire Congress could operate like that, discussing national issues constructively, in a spirit of mutual affection and respect. Maybe someday we will.

But until that great day arrives we had better look to ourselves, not to politics, to build the America of our dreams. In my mind, this book is ultimately about you and me. It is a call for each of us to consider the works of our heroes, decide what our gifts are—and use them. We don't have to move mountains, but we do need to join, in some way, the quiet revolution that is battling for the soul of America.

What is your gift? How can you best serve? Are you ready to take the first step? For those who do, there may be no turning back, because even as you help others, and help your country, you are most of all helping yourself lead a richer, more rewarding life.

The most wonderful thing about the heroes in this book is that they are really just ordinary people who one day decided to act. You can too. Join the struggle. It won't be easy. There are bound to be failures and setbacks. But we will all be happier working toward a common goal than watching passively from the sidelines. Find your special gift and use it. Remember, courage is contagious.

ADDRESSES

Some of the organizations and individuals written about in this book asked that their addresses be listed, to enable readers to write for more information or to make donations.

Albert Lexie, Apartment 604, Westgate Manor, Monessen, PA 15062

American Hospice Foundation, 1130 Connecticut Avenue, N.W., Suite 700, Washington, DC 20036

Angels' Place, 25140 Lahser Road, Suite 232, Southfield, MI 48034

Association to Benefit Children, 419 East 86th Street, New York, NY 10028

Barclay School, 2900 Barclay, Baltimore, MD 21218

Clown Care Unit, Big Apple Circus, 35 West 35th Street, New York, NY 10001

Concord Counseling Services, 924 Eastwind Drive, Westerville, OH 43081

Happy Helpers for the Homeless, 403-A Old Stage Road, Glen Burnie, MD 21061

Holocaust Rescuer Foundation, P.O. Box 1214, Laguna Beach, CA 92652

Hospice Care of Oklahoma, Suite 1100, 1211 N. Shartel, Oklahoma City, OK 73103

National Interfaith Hospitality Network, 71 Summit Avenue, Summit, NJ 07901

Piney Woods Country Life School, P.O. Box 99, Piney Woods, MS 39148

Rheedlen Centers for Children & Families, 2770 Broadway, New York, NY 10025

Schools on Wheels, P.O. Box 2283, Malibu, CA 90265

Volunteers in Medicine, 29 Old Ford Drive, Hilton Head Island, SC 29926

Now in his eighth term representing central Ohio's Twelfth Congressional District, House Budget Committee Chairman John Kasich has become a nationally recognized leader of the Republican Party. Chief negotiator for the House of Representatives as Congress and President Clinton reached agreement on a plan to balance the budget by 2002, he also chaired the House-Senate committee that wrote the final version of the Welfare Reform Law in 1996. One of the most sought-after speakers in the Republican Party, Kasich has been profiled on "60 Minutes" and appears often on "Meet the Press," "Larry King Live" and other network programs to discuss national issues. *Newsweek* named him one of its "100 People for the Next Century."